home decorating workbooks

dried flowers

home decorating workbooks

dried flowers

Hilary Mandleberg

designs by
Stephen Woodhams

photography by Simon Brown

RYLAND
PETERS
& SMALL

First published in Great Britain in 1999
by Ryland Peters & Small
Cavendish House
51–55 Mortimer Street
London W1N 7TD

Publishing Director **Anne Ryland**

Head of Design **Gabriella Le Grazie**

Designer **Sally Powell**

Editorial Assistant **Maddalena Bastianelli**

Production **Rosanna Dickinson**

Illustrator **Michael Hill**

10 9 8 7 6 5 4 3 2 1

Produced by Sun Fung Offset Binding Co., Ltd
Printed in China

ISBN: 1 84172 005 4

A CIP catalogue record for this book is
available from the British Library.

contents

DRIED FLOWERS HAVE BEEN AROUND FOR AS LONG AS I CAN REMEMBER but people so often think of them gathering dust in gloomy corners of country cottages that they would not dream of having them in their own homes. It is quite a challenge to introduce them into contemporary settings, but I hope that this book will prove that it can be done.

If you think about dried flowers at all, you perhaps consider them as something to have in the house in autumn or winter, to supplement the limited fresh flowers available at that time of year, or you might be bold enough to think of offering dried red roses to a loved one on Valentine's Day. But to prove to you just how versatile dried flowers can be, I have chosen to take you through the whole year, suggesting ways to use them and showing how appropriate these much-maligned creatures can be, whatever the season.

In this fast-paced age, you may be one of the many who don't have the time or inclination to buy and arrange fresh flowers on a regular basis. If, so, a beautiful, long-lasting dried flower arrangement is just the thing to lift your spirits when you come home after a long, hectic day A successful dried-flower arrangement can add the finishing touch to and strengthen the impact of any room. It can enhance a colour scheme, pick up the mood of the furnishings, underline the textures of fabrics and furniture, or emphasize the scale of a room and its contents. And what is more, it will easily last four or five years, by which time you will probably be thinking about redecorating anyway.

An arrangement of dried flowers can also serve as a quick and easy table decoration at an impromptu dinner party, or it can make the perfect gift. I nearly always keep a small wrapped dried arrangement in the house on standby, in case I'm suddenly invited out to dinner and need to take a present with me. And in case you still need convincing, you

should know that recent methods of drying and preserving plant material mean that it now retains its beautiful bright colours and textures in a way that was unheard of just a few years ago. Roses and lavender look as fresh as the day they were picked. Preserved foliages could have come straight from the tree. Freeze-dried fruits and vegetables look almost good enough to eat. Even ordinary green carpet moss keeps its colour for years on end.

The optimum atmosphere for keeping dried arrangements at their best is a warm, dry one. Damp conditions will shorten their life, and if the air is too cool, some dried plant material will start to sweat. And if you need to remove any dust that has settled on your dried arrangement, just waft a hairdryer on a cold setting over it.

Safety is also a consideration where dried material is concerned. If your arrangement is going to stand near an open fire where sparks might fly, or if it is to include lighted candles, then I would always advise you to spray the dried material with a fire-retardant liquid.

And now to the arrangements. Just as fashion dictates that displays of fresh flowers move towards cleaner, simpler lines, so the same is true of dried flowers. This, I think, is the key to ensuring that dried flower arrangements look good in contemporary settings. What is more, there is now a huge selection of dried tropical material on the market. With its graphic lines, it looks as if it has been specially grown to suit a minimalist loft apartment or a limestone-lined bathroom. Seashells look great with dried flowers, too, but check with your supplier that the shells have come from countries where efforts are being made to regulate the shell trade, otherwise you could be contributing to the destruction of marine life. This book shows much of this newly available material in use, together with a mass of the more traditional material we know and love – peonies, dahlias, marigolds, pine cones, and so on.

I hope you will find plenty to inspire you within these pages and that they will give you the confidence to adapt my designs to suit other material if you wish. I also hope that if, in the past, you decided that dried arrangements were not for you, perhaps, after reading this book, you will reconsider. Welcome back!

Stephen Woodhams

left and below The wealth of dried material that is available gives me the opportunity for some rather unusual designs. Here I have used bell cups painted duck-egg-blue to tone with their blue vase. The spiral positioning of the bell cups complements their lovely shape. This is an arrangement that looks good from any angle.

above The intensity of colour of this globe of rich yellow rose heads contrasts glowingly with the muted green freeze-dried moss lining the glass vase. The effect is sublimely spring-like.
right Pussy willow is one of the joys of spring. You can buy it ready dried or dry it yourself by simply standing it in a vase without water. It's very important to pick it while it's still at its silvery bud stage, before the stamens emerge.

left Painted red, green and yellow, these calabash pods remind me of sweet peppers, so it seemed natural to put them in a wire basket kitchen container.
below left Yellow and grey is one of my favourite colour combinations. Here, I capitalize on it with square galvanized pots filled with yellow rose heads. They add a touch of softness to a modern stainless-steel kitchen.
below right Often a container suggests an arrangement. In this case, I couldn't resist the charm of an intensely, opaquely green vase. There was no choice but to fill it with dyed green thistles.

spring

It's all been said before, but there's no doubt that spring is when we shed our winter woollies and look forward to a season of lengthening days, the touch of the sun on our skin and a fresh new start. It's the same in nature. In the warmth of the sun, bare branches miraculously sprout furry catkins, tight, fat buds unfurl into yellow-green leaves and dormant lawns suddenly demand their first haircut of the year. As this spring collection goes to show, dried flowers are just as capable of capturing the spirit of the season as fresh ones. Choose from revitalizing greens and yellows or clear sky-blue, and position your designs to make the most of the magical light of spring.

sunny dahlia topiary

Although dahlias are usually thought of as late-summer flowers,
the sunny open faces of these make me think of an Easter
breakfast of fried eggs 'sunny side up'. In a couple of years'
time, when the flowers eventually fade, you can create
a whole new look with a spray of gold paint.

materials & equipment

pot, 20 cm (8 in) high x 18 cm (7 in) diameter

25–35 birch twigs

2 stems dogwood, to fit around pot

1 block dry floral foam, 55 x 32 x 23 cm (22 x 13 x 9 in)

10–12 bamboo canes, approximately 45 cm (18 in) long

1 ball dry floral foam, 16 cm (6 in) diameter

dried lichen, to cover

140–160 dried dahlia heads

trimming knife • glue • medium-gauge stub wires • floristry knife • raffia

7 Gouge a hole in the centre of the foam-filled pot and in the foam ball, then push one end of the bamboo-cane bundle deep into the pot and the other end into the ball. The raffia ties should now be hidden by the floral foam.

8 Glue the pieces of dried lichen to cover the ball of floral foam.

9 Glue the dahlia heads on top of the lichen, allowing the lichen to show through in places.

10 Finish off by covering the surface of the foam-filled pot with more lichen, held in place with bent stub wires.

1 Cut the birch twigs into 21 cm (8½ in) lengths. Using a trimming knife and always working away from your body, taper the lower half to one-third of the cut twigs so they will fit snugly around the pot. If you use a straight-sided pot, this will not be necessary.

2 Glue the tapered twigs to the outside of the pot. Position them closely to one another. You may have to taper the last twig further to ensure a good fit.

3 Cut the dogwood into two lengths, to fit around the top and bottom of the pot and allowing 2.5 cm (1 in) for an overlap. Decide which will be the back of the pot. If you tapered the last twig to fit, this should be at the back.

4 Dab some glue 1 cm (⅜ in) above the bottom edge of the pot, then wrap the shorter length of dogwood around, overlapping it at the back. Push a medium-gauge stub wire behind each of the overlaps, then bend the wires forward and twist their ends tightly together to hold the dogwood in place. Trim the ends of the wire and repeat for the top edge.

5 Using a knife, cut the floral foam to fit inside the pot. It should sit about 2.5 cm (1 in) below the top of the pot.

6 Tie the bamboo canes together top and bottom to make a bundle, using lengths of raffia.

chinese chequers

I like to think of this design as more of a floor-standing sculpture than a flower arrangement. With its strong vertical lines, it punctuates a row of floor cushions in a novel and eyecatching manner. The unique mosaic-effect ceramic container was crying out for unusual plant material with a contemporary feel: geometrically arranged snakegrass and Chinese reed in toning shades of green were the perfect choice.

materials & equipment

ceramic container, 23 x 18 x 18 cm (9 x 7 x 7 in)

1 block dry floral foam, 55 x 32 x 23 cm (22 x 13 x 9 in)

16 stems dried Chinese reed

8 stems dried snakegrass

dried lichen, dyed green, to cover

knife • floristry scissors • raffia • medium-gauge stub wires

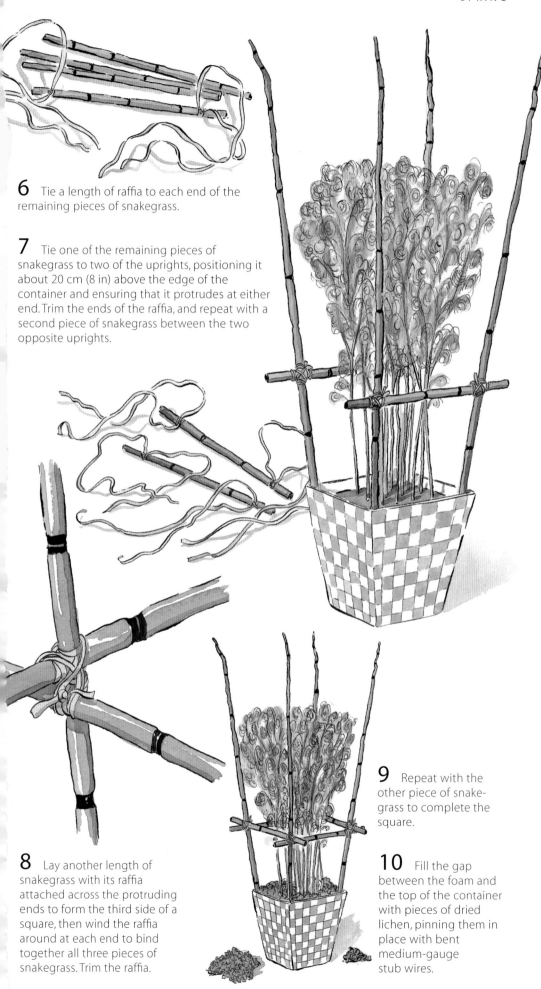

6 Tie a length of raffia to each end of the remaining pieces of snakegrass.

7 Tie one of the remaining pieces of snakegrass to two of the uprights, positioning it about 20 cm (8 in) above the edge of the container and ensuring that it protrudes at either end. Trim the ends of the raffia, and repeat with a second piece of snakegrass between the two opposite uprights.

8 Lay another length of snakegrass with its raffia attached across the protruding ends to form the third side of a square, then wind the raffia around at each end to bind together all three pieces of snakegrass. Trim the raffia.

9 Repeat with the other piece of snakegrass to complete the square.

10 Fill the gap between the foam and the top of the container with pieces of dried lichen, pinning them in place with bent medium-gauge stub wires.

18

1 Use the sharp knife to cut the block of floral foam to fit the container. The foam should sit about 2.5 cm (1in) below the top of the container.

2 Using scissors, trim the Chinese reed to 50 cm (20 in).

3 Push the Chinese reed into the foam in four rows of four.

4 Trim four stems of snakegrass to 70 cm (28 in) and four to 30 cm (12 in).

5 Position the four longer pieces of snakegrass in the corners of the container.

instructions under flap ➤

clouds in a tree

With their dense mass of tightly packed and shaded flower heads
'suspended' among the lovely, loose stems of contorted willow,
cloud trees always remind me of those beautiful clear spring days,
when the sky is an amazing crisp blue, and scudding puffy white
clouds look as if they have been caught up in the branches
of the trees. The effect lasts just moments but here,
with a little imagination, it is captured forever.

materials & equipment

inner container, 32 cm (13 in) high x 23 cm (9 in) diameter

outer container, 35 cm (14 in) high x 25 cm (10 in) diameter

3 stems contorted willow

1 block dry floral foam, 55 x 32 x 23 cm (22 x 13 x 9 in)

5 cm (2 in) chicken wire, to cover

300–350 dried yellow roses

Spanish moss, to cover

dried lichen, to cover

trowel • quick-drying cement • knife • wire cutters
medium-gauge stub wires • secateurs

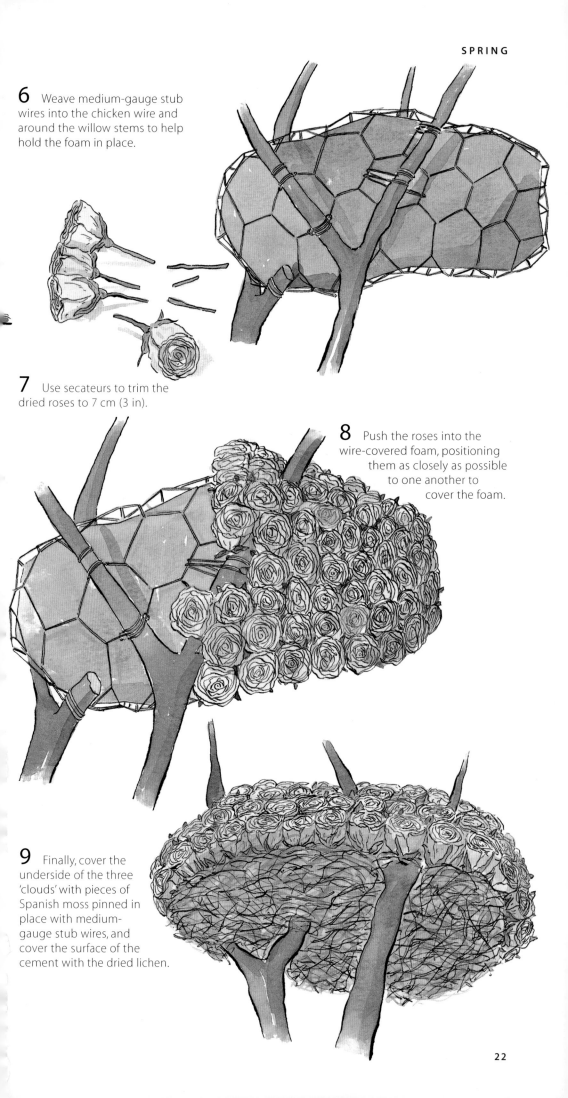

6 Weave medium-gauge stub wires into the chicken wire and around the willow stems to help hold the foam in place.

7 Use secateurs to trim the dried roses to 7 cm (3 in).

8 Push the roses into the wire-covered foam, positioning them as closely as possible to one another to cover the foam.

9 Finally, cover the underside of the three 'clouds' with pieces of Spanish moss pinned in place with medium-gauge stub wires, and cover the surface of the cement with the dried lichen.

1 Following the manufacturer's instructions, make a quick-drying cement mixture and pour it into the inner container.

2 Working quickly, stand the stems of contorted willow in the cement and hold them in place while it sets. Stand the inner container in the outer, display container.

3 Using the knife, cut the block of foam into 25 cm (10 in), 18 cm (7 in) and 12 cm (5 in) lengths, then shape the three blocks into roughly ovoid shapes with flattened bases.

4 Wrap the foam pieces in the chicken wire, cutting into the wire at intervals around its edges with wire cutters so you can fold it snugly in place.

5 Position the pieces of foam so they nestle among the stems like clouds caught in the branches of a tree. If necessary, trim the stems of the willow to support the foam securely. Position the largest piece of foam about a quarter of the way up from the base, the smallest about a quarter of the way down from the top, and the medium one between the two.

boxing clever

Being a gardener at heart, I am especially fond of this dried-flower arrangement. It looks just like the sort of boxwood topiary you might find growing in an elegant garden. A pair of these either side of a fireplace or, in miniature, on the mantelpiece, would be very striking. Green spray paint keeps the arrangement looking fresh. At Christmas time, you could use gold or silver paint. Who needs any other Christmas tree?

materials & equipment

inner container, 20 cm (8 in) high x 15 cm (6 in) diameter

outer container, 25 cm (10 in) high x 20 cm (8 in) diameter

birch pole, 70 cm (28 in) long x 4 cm (1½ in) diameter

1 block dry floral foam, 55 x 32 x 23 cm (22 x 13 x 9 in)

5 cm (2 in) chicken wire, to cover

500–600 sprigs boxwood

green spray-paint

white gravel, to cover

knife • ruler • pencil • bamboo cane, 2.5 cm (1 in) diameter • trowel
quick-drying cement • florist's tape • wire cutters • heavy-gauge stub wires
reel wire • secateurs • floristry scissors • medium-gauge stub wires
masking tape • plastic sheeting

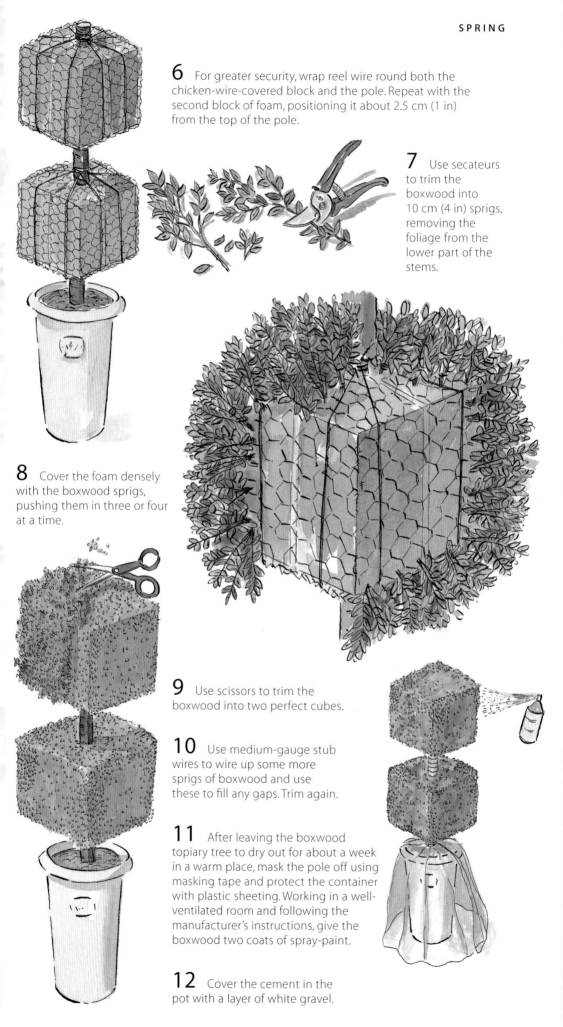

6 For greater security, wrap reel wire round both the chicken-wire-covered block and the pole. Repeat with the second block of foam, positioning it about 2.5 cm (1 in) from the top of the pole.

7 Use secateurs to trim the boxwood into 10 cm (4 in) sprigs, removing the foliage from the lower part of the stems.

8 Cover the foam densely with the boxwood sprigs, pushing them in three or four at a time.

9 Use scissors to trim the boxwood into two perfect cubes.

10 Use medium-gauge stub wires to wire up some more sprigs of boxwood and use these to fill any gaps. Trim again.

11 After leaving the boxwood topiary tree to dry out for about a week in a warm place, mask the pole off using masking tape and protect the container with plastic sheeting. Working in a well-ventilated room and following the manufacturer's instructions, give the boxwood two coats of spray-paint.

12 Cover the cement in the pot with a layer of white gravel.

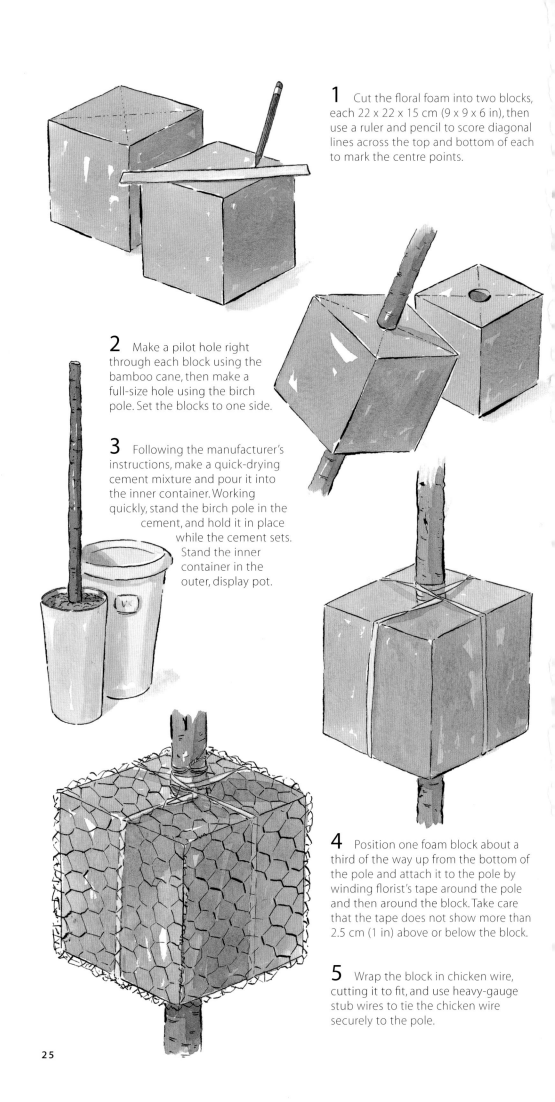

1 Cut the floral foam into two blocks, each 22 x 22 x 15 cm (9 x 9 x 6 in), then use a ruler and pencil to score diagonal lines across the top and bottom of each to mark the centre points.

2 Make a pilot hole right through each block using the bamboo cane, then make a full-size hole using the birch pole. Set the blocks to one side.

3 Following the manufacturer's instructions, make a quick-drying cement mixture and pour it into the inner container. Working quickly, stand the birch pole in the cement, and hold it in place while the cement sets. Stand the inner container in the outer, display pot.

4 Position one foam block about a third of the way up from the bottom of the pole and attach it to the pole by winding florist's tape around the pole and then around the block. Take care that the tape does not show more than 2.5 cm (1 in) above or below the block.

5 Wrap the block in chicken wire, cutting it to fit, and use heavy-gauge stub wires to tie the chicken wire securely to the pole.

sensual indulgence

Stylized but warm is the way I would describe this combination of classic dried roses and heady, scented lavender. With the lavender beautifully magnified by the glass vase, the arrangement brings a touch of softness to a stainless-steel kitchen. Though it looks striking on its own, you could try arranging a matching pair on a low table, bathed in lamplight. A circular bowl filled with a mound of rich yellow lemons would be the finishing touch.

materials & equipment

glass vase, 40 x 18 x 18 cm (15 x 7 x 7 in)

1 block dry floral foam, 55 x 32 x 23 cm (22 x 13 x 9 in)

dried lavender, to fill

1 ball dry floral foam, 20 cm (8 in) diameter

wooden stick, 40 cm (15 in) long x 1.5 cm (½ in) diameter

150–200 dried yellow roses

knife • secateurs

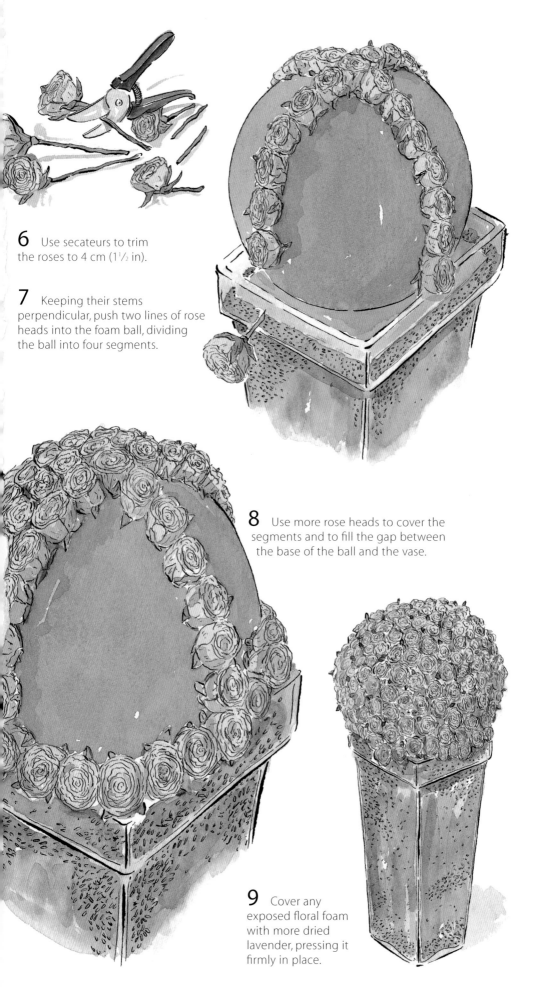

6 Use secateurs to trim the roses to 4 cm (1½ in).

7 Keeping their stems perpendicular, push two lines of rose heads into the foam ball, dividing the ball into four segments.

8 Use more rose heads to cover the segments and to fill the gap between the base of the ball and the vase.

9 Cover any exposed floral foam with more dried lavender, pressing it firmly in place.

1 Using the knife, shape the block of floral foam to fit inside the vase, leaving enough space for the dried lavender to be poured around the sides. The floral foam core makes the project more economical and gives the arrangement stability.

2 Sprinkle a layer of dried lavender in the bottom of the vase and position the shaped floral foam on top.

3 Pour more lavender around the foam to fill the vase.

4 Push about one-third of the stick into the ball of floral foam.

5 Push the rest of the stick with the ball attached into the floral foam in the vase so the ball is resting on top of the foam block.

left Regimental roses combine with leisurely lychees to make an unusual display in shades of pink and red. The prickly skin of the dried lychees magnified by the glass vase is a pleasure to see.

below Dainty, feathery love-in-a-mist is one of summer's most delightful flowers. It dries beautifully. Here it has been made into a simple wreath which, I think, would look terrific hanging on the wall of someone's kitchen.

summer

Blooming in every colour of the rainbow, summer flowers have that extra burst of energy that we all feel when the days are long and the sun is high in the sky. If you want to dry your own flowers, this is your busiest time of year. Capture the fizz and heat of summer with dried roses and lavender, sun-baked wood, and exuberant, rustling armfuls of oats.

above Looking and feeling as if they were delicately carved from wood, these dried protea heads make the perfect accompaniment to a rusty round container. With their fabulous centres, they remind me of sunflowers or gerberas, but texturally they are in a class of their own.

left This simple arrangement of assorted dried material has a very tropical feel, as if the ingredients have been gathered from the hard-baked earth of an equatorial village. Pieces of coco shell jostle with Amazon seppecioa husks, a palm seed head and spheres made from panchu reed.

left I usually make corn sheaves, but this oat sheaf has a lovely loose feel. It would bring the country to an urban kitchen. Small sheaves with name tags tied on make unusual place cards.
below A plateau of dried lavender in a square pot suits a modern or traditional space.

above The sheer overwhelming abundance of rose heads and lavender in this metre- (3-foot) tall arrangement makes me dream of the exuberance of summer. Stand it on the floor as I have done, or be ultra-daring and put it on a console table flanked by a pair of lamps. It cannot fail to impress.
right I love the sexy curves of this white vase so chose the twisty, curving, beautifully grained banana sticks to complement them. Dried naturally in the sun, banana sticks remind me of pieces of driftwood washed up on a beach. I think this is one of my most exotic, sensual arrangements.

the bounty of the sea

What a breathtaking wedding present this would be for the owners of a seaside home or a grand beach hut. It really conjures up the spirit of the seashore. Add an extra dimension to it by sprinkling the arrangement with a fragrant essential oil and breathing in the magic.

materials & equipment

light-coloured flatweave basket, 60 x 30 x 20 cm (24 x 12 x 8 in)

5 cm (2 in) chicken wire, 2 m (80 in) x 20 cm (8 in)

dried sphagnum moss, for garland

60 dried liquorice root sticks

80 stems split bamboo

50 stems dried canella berries

60 dried and bleached thorn apple fruits

60 assorted shells, including four large shells, with long spines, that can be used as 'anchors'

5 starfish

dried reindeer moss, to finish

medium-gauge stub wires • secateurs • approximately 4 m (4¼ yd) cotton string
knife • glue

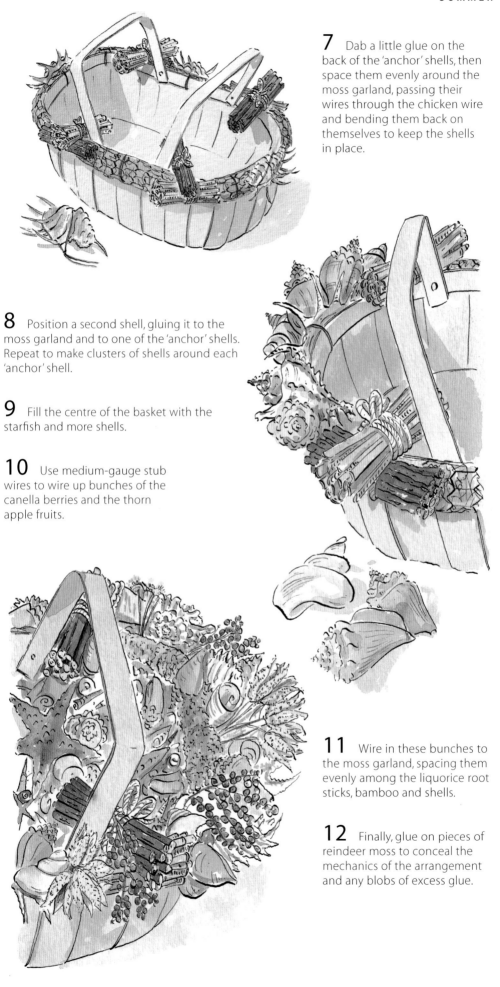

7 Dab a little glue on the back of the 'anchor' shells, then space them evenly around the moss garland, passing their wires through the chicken wire and bending them back on themselves to keep the shells in place.

8 Position a second shell, gluing it to the moss garland and to one of the 'anchor' shells. Repeat to make clusters of shells around each 'anchor' shell.

9 Fill the centre of the basket with the starfish and more shells.

10 Use medium-gauge stub wires to wire up bunches of the canella berries and the thorn apple fruits.

11 Wire in these bunches to the moss garland, spacing them evenly among the liquorice root sticks, bamboo and shells.

12 Finally, glue on pieces of reindeer moss to conceal the mechanics of the arrangement and any blobs of excess glue.

1 Lay the strip of chicken wire on a flat surface and position the moss down its centre, keeping the edges of the chicken wire free.

2 Fold the edges of the chicken wire over to enclose the moss, forming a moss garland.

3 Attach the moss garland to the top edge of the basket, securing it at intervals with medium-gauge stub wires.

4 Use secateurs to trim the liquorice root sticks, split bamboo, stems of canella berries and thorn apple fruits to 20 cm (8 in). Tie the liquorice root sticks into four equal-sized bundles using medium-gauge stub wires. Leave the ends of the wires long. Repeat for the split bamboo. Conceal the wire holding the bundles with a covering of string wrapped several times around and finished with a small bow.

5 Use the long ends of the wire to attach the bundles of liquorice root sticks and bamboo evenly around the top of the basket. Push the wires into the moss garland and bend them back on themselves to hold the bundles in place. Place the bundles in pairs, one bundle at a 90-degree angle to the other.

6 Wire up the four large, jagged 'anchor' shells by threading a medium-gauge stub wire between their spines and twisting the long ends of the wire together. Help to keep the wire in place with a dab or two of glue.

summer herbal

Bring the scent and colour of summer into your home with this magnificent garland of traditional herbs and flowers. Lavender, oregano, marjoram and cinnamon waft on the air, while muted pinks, mauves and greens splashed with bright gold are a feast for the eye. No matter where you hang it, this garland is sure to win compliments and will remind you of the warmth and colour of summer long after garden flowers have faded.

materials & equipment

5 cm (2 in) chicken wire, 22 cm (9 in) x 75 cm (30 in)

dried sphagnum moss, for garland, plus extra to cover gaps

40–50 stems dried ambrosinia

40–50 stems dried oregano

approximately 7 m (7 yd) seagrass twine

80–100 stems each dried marjoram, linseed, heather, lavender

15–20 stems dried pink pepper berries

56 cinnamon sticks

20–25 dried marigolds

secateurs • medium-gauge stub wires • heavy-gauge stub wires
fine-gauge stub wires • glue

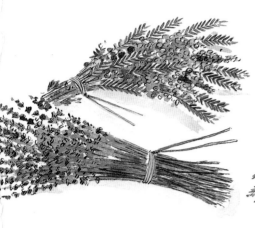

8 Trim the marjoram, linseed, heather, lavender and pink pepper berries, and wire them into bunches in the same way.

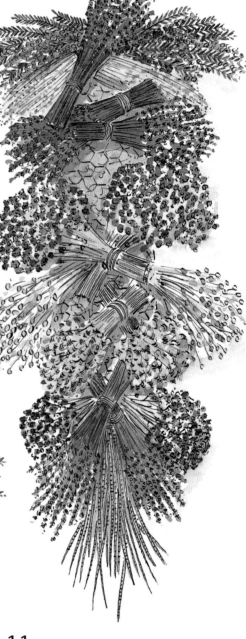

9 Wire these bunches to the garland, positioning them to ensure a good balance of colours and textures.

10 Use heavy-gauge stub wires to wire up eight bundles of cinnamon sticks and attach them to the garland in a criss-cross pattern.

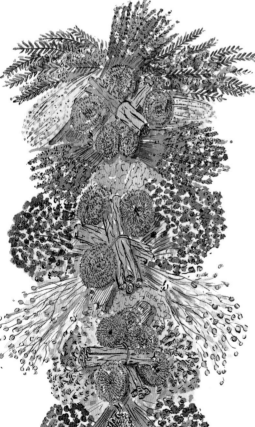

11 Use fine-gauge stub wires to wire up the individual marigold flowers, then arrange them in groups among the other material.

12 Cover any gaps in the arrangement with pieces of moss attached with glue.

13 To make a hanging loop, pass a heavy-gauge stub wire through half the thickness of the garland at the back, turn it back on itself, then twist the two free ends together.

ocean-going peonies

Classical meets nautical and the result is an unusual marriage.
Peonies epitomize summer, so add some chunky white cotton
rope and you have an image of a hot sunny day in a garden,
with herbaceous borders running down to the
riverbank and pleasure boats sailing by.

materials & equipment

container, 25 cm (10 in) high x 18 cm (7 in) diameter

wire urn, 42.5 cm (17 in) high x 32 cm (13 in) diameter

approximately 5 m (6 yd) cotton rope x 1.5 cm (½ in) diameter

1 block dry floral foam, 55 x 32 x 23 cm (22 x 13 x 9 in)

75–85 dried peonies

15 stems dried pink pepper berries

glue • knife • secateurs • medium-gauge stub wires

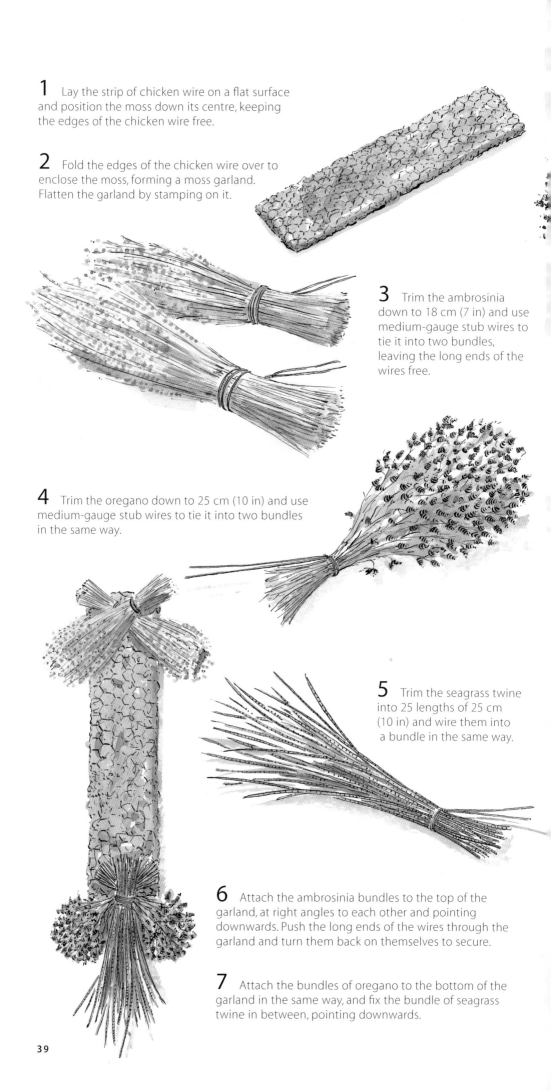

1 Lay the strip of chicken wire on a flat surface and position the moss down its centre, keeping the edges of the chicken wire free.

2 Fold the edges of the chicken wire over to enclose the moss, forming a moss garland. Flatten the garland by stamping on it.

3 Trim the ambrosinia down to 18 cm (7 in) and use medium-gauge stub wires to tie it into two bundles, leaving the long ends of the wires free.

4 Trim the oregano down to 25 cm (10 in) and use medium-gauge stub wires to tie it into two bundles in the same way.

5 Trim the seagrass twine into 25 lengths of 25 cm (10 in) and wire them into a bundle in the same way.

6 Attach the ambrosinia bundles to the top of the garland, at right angles to each other and pointing downwards. Push the long ends of the wires through the garland and turn them back on themselves to secure.

7 Attach the bundles of oregano to the bottom of the garland in the same way, and fix the bundle of seagrass twine in between, pointing downwards.

6 Starting at the centre of the container, push the peonies into the foam, arranging them so their heads are closely packed.

7 Leaving the top edge of the urn free of flowers and trimming the peonies further if necessary, continue positioning them until they form a soft dome shape.

8 Wire up the stems of the pink pepper berries by bending medium-gauge stub wires into hairpin shapes with one leg longer than the other. Hold the bent wire against the stem and wind the long leg around the stem and the other leg of wire. Use the wired-up berries to fill the gap between the peonies and the top of the urn.

sun-bleached grasses

Pale but interesting. Bleached bone-white, this composition of dried grasses and seed heads embodies a pared-down view of nature that I find immensely satisfying. Grouping the different elements in tiers in this way makes for a strong, contemporary statement with loads of impact.

materials & equipment

frosted glass vase, 30 cm (12 in) high x 22 cm (9 in) diameter

1 block dry floral foam, 55 x 32 x 23 cm (22 x 13 x 9 in)

dried reindeer moss, to fill

120–140 stems dried wheat

170–180 stems dried phalaris

60–70 dried poppy seed heads

knife • raffia

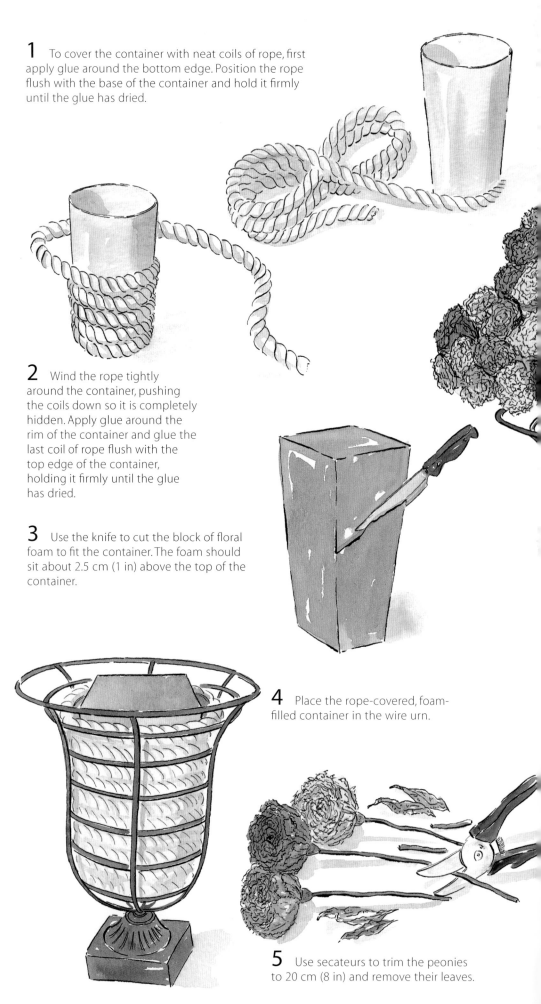

1 To cover the container with neat coils of rope, first apply glue around the bottom edge. Position the rope flush with the base of the container and hold it firmly until the glue has dried.

2 Wind the rope tightly around the container, pushing the coils down so it is completely hidden. Apply glue around the rim of the container and glue the last coil of rope flush with the top edge of the container, holding it firmly until the glue has dried.

3 Use the knife to cut the block of floral foam to fit the container. The foam should sit about 2.5 cm (1 in) above the top of the container.

4 Place the rope-covered, foam-filled container in the wire urn.

5 Use secateurs to trim the peonies to 20 cm (8 in) and remove their leaves.

4 Tie the wheat into a bundle, fastening it about two-thirds of the way down with raffia.

5 Push the bundle of wheat into the centre of the block of floral foam.

6 Arrange the phalaris in a circle around the wheat to form a dense mass of heads that conceals the raffia tying the wheat bundle. Push the phalaris into the floral foam two or three stems at a time.

7 Finally, arrange the poppy seed heads around the base of the wheat and the phalaris, pushing them in so the surface of the floral foam is concealed.

1 Use the knife to cut the block of floral foam to fit the vase, leaving a gap of about 2.5 cm (1 in) between the foam and the sides of the vase, and a gap of 2.5 cm (1 in) between the top of the foam and the top of the vase.

2 Fill the space between the foam and the sides of the vase with pieces of reindeer moss.

3 Trim the stems of wheat to 50 cm (20 in), the phalaris to 34 cm (14 in), and the poppy seed heads to 10 cm (4 in).

in a whirl

What better way to bring the scent of summer into your home
than with a spiral of massed marjoram flowers? They have an
amazing perfume when crushed. As this summer-flowering herb
has naturally dense clusters of flowers, it is ideal for using in
a closely packed design like this one. The opulent effect makes
me think of a lavish fur tightly wrapped around the
shoulders of a rich, glamorous woman.

materials & equipment

inner container, 37 cm (15 in) high x 25 cm (10 in) diameter

outer container, 45 cm (18 in) high x 30 cm (12 in) diameter

birch pole, 90 cm (36 in) long x 4 cm (1½ in) diameter

5 cm (2 in) chicken wire, 110 cm (44 in) x 32 cm (13 in), tapering to 15 cm (6 in)

dried sphagnum moss, for garland

250–300 sprigs dried marjoram

pebbles, to cover

trowel • quick-drying cement • wire cutters • reel wire • heavy-gauge stub wires
secateurs • medium-gauge stub wires

7 Wrap the garland around the pole in a spiral, attaching it at the bottom with more heavy-gauge stub wires.

8 Use the secateurs to trim the marjoram to 15 cm (6 in) and tie it in clusters with medium-gauge stub wires, leaving the ends of the wires free.

9 Starting at the top of the spiral, secure the marjoram clusters by laying one flat on the garland, pushing its wires under the chicken wire, then turning the wires back on themselves. Lay the next cluster so it conceals the stems of the first, and continue until the whole spiral is covered with marjoram.

10 Complete the arrangement by concealing the surface of the cement with the pebbles.

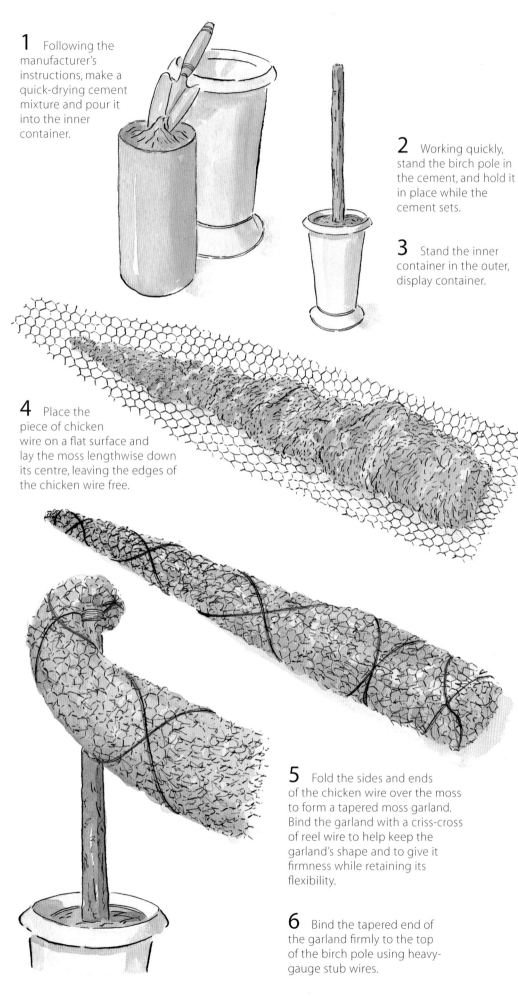

1 Following the manufacturer's instructions, make a quick-drying cement mixture and pour it into the inner container.

2 Working quickly, stand the birch pole in the cement, and hold it in place while the cement sets.

3 Stand the inner container in the outer, display container.

4 Place the piece of chicken wire on a flat surface and lay the moss lengthwise down its centre, leaving the edges of the chicken wire free.

5 Fold the sides and ends of the chicken wire over the moss to form a tapered moss garland. Bind the garland with a criss-cross of reel wire to help keep the garland's shape and to give it firmness while retaining its flexibility.

6 Bind the tapered end of the garland firmly to the top of the birch pole using heavy-gauge stub wires.

left The glorious texture of these badam pods shows through the light yellow wash of paint that has been applied to them. Their wonderful sculpted form makes an unforgettably graphic display.

below One of my favourite fresh foliages is papyrus, so I was thrilled to discover the dried version – a gentle sage green colour – on sale. A mixture of the dried heads plus some on stems is bold and brave.

right Freeze-dried roses are so flawless that I have to touch them to check they are not fresh. This gold-effect spun-metal candlestick caught my eye immediately. It looked great with the chunky church candle, but somehow didn't seem quite finished. The answer was to add a double garland of freeze-dried yellow roses. They make just the right link between the candle and its holder.

far right Many arrangements are bought off the peg from my shop and I have no idea if they will suit the locations they are destined for or not, but this is a perfect example of one that was commissioned to suit a particular place. Here, an enormous cone of freeze-dried cream roses in an unusual tortoiseshell container stands on a stem made from a cluster of bamboo. The whole arrangement is at one with its mellow surroundings – a cream and white room with luxuriant carpet, oatmeal suede chairs and a white leather-covered trunk serving as a coffee table.

left Pared-down dried arrangements are the perfect partners for minimalism and natural, organic materials. What could be more contemporary than this simple bunch of dried reeds laid on a limestone hearth?
below left Bleaching strips an object down to its very essence. Set against a chocolate-brown wall, this triple-layer arrangement of spheres made from bleached reeds on cane stems really concentrates the mind.
below right Classic roses are given a contemporary edge in a glass bowl lined with cinnamon sticks. Simplicity is the key.

autumn

Holidays are over and it's reluctantly back to school. Summer's heat has passed, the days begin to shorten again, and vivid brights give way to mellow yellows and spice-trail shades of oatmeal, buff, biscuit and ginger. This is harvest time – the season of fragrant grasses, rich brown nuts and succulent berries. As evenings close in, become a hermit. Withdraw from the world to your own private space. Make a steaming mug of creamy, frothy coffee, immerse yourself in an engrossing novel and bask in the gentle amber glow of candlelight with a contented fat tortoiseshell cat on your lap.

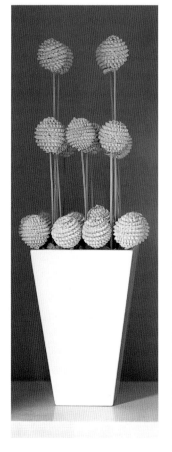

glacé fruits

As autumn turns to winter, cheery preserved fruits bring a little
colour back into our lives. In this arrangement I have used simple
rounds of glowing sliced citrus fruits to hide the mechanics,
complemented by jewelled globes of dried oranges and
mandarins gushing out of the top of the vase. The gnarled
stems of the contorted willow make a stark contrast
to the opulent shapes and colours of the fruits.

materials & equipment

glass vase, 37 x 18 x 18 cm (15 x 7 x 7 in)

1 block dry floral foam, 55 x 32 x 23 cm (22 x 13 x 9 in)

75–85 dried citrus slices

2 or 3 stems contorted willow

40–50 assorted dried split mandarins, and split orange and green oranges

knife • secateurs • medium-gauge stub wires

5 Wire up the mandarins and the orange and green oranges by passing a medium-gauge stub wire through one of the splits in the fruit and out through another. Twist the ends of the wire together.

6 Starting around the base of the contorted willow, push the wired-up fruits into the floral foam.

7 Continue covering the surface of the foam with wired-up fruits ensuring a good mix of size and colour.

8 Finish the arrangement by positioning wired-up fruits around the edge of the foam to cover the gap between the foam and the top edge of the vase.

1 Use the knife to cut the block of floral foam to fit inside the glass vase, leaving about 2.5 cm (1 in) all round between the foam and the sides of the vase. The block should sit about 2.5 cm (1 in) below the top of the vase.

2 Place the foam in the vase and fill the space between it and the sides of the vase with the citrus slices.

3 Use secateurs to trim the stems of contorted willow to about 75 cm (30 in).

4 Push about one-third of the length of the stems of contorted willow firmly into the centre of the block of floral foam.

gentleman's club

In its bedroom setting, this strictly formal arrangement in muted autumnal shades oozes masculinity. Knowing where an arrangement is to be placed and the character of the home-owner is usually the starting point for my designs. Here I have complemented the colours of the dried plant material with a severe creamware pot. The grain of the wooden candlesticks picks up the nuts and cream theme to perfection.

materials & equipment

container, 37 x 18 x 18 cm (15 x 7 x 7 in)

1 block dry floral foam, 55 x 32 x 23 cm (22 x 13 x 9 in)

4–5 dried assegai sticks

16–20 dried bulrushes

16 thick-stemmed reeds

dried lichen, to cover

knife • secateurs • raffia • medium-gauge stub wires

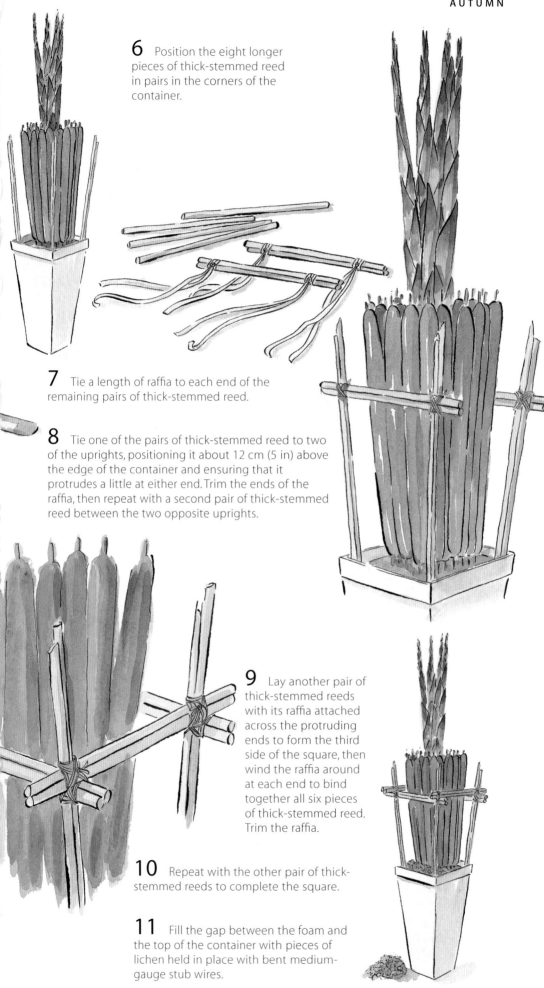

6 Position the eight longer pieces of thick-stemmed reed in pairs in the corners of the container.

7 Tie a length of raffia to each end of the remaining pairs of thick-stemmed reed.

8 Tie one of the pairs of thick-stemmed reed to two of the uprights, positioning it about 12 cm (5 in) above the edge of the container and ensuring that it protrudes a little at either end. Trim the ends of the raffia, then repeat with a second pair of thick-stemmed reed between the two opposite uprights.

9 Lay another pair of thick-stemmed reeds with its raffia attached across the protruding ends to form the third side of the square, then wind the raffia around at each end to bind together all six pieces of thick-stemmed reed. Trim the raffia.

10 Repeat with the other pair of thick-stemmed reeds to complete the square.

11 Fill the gap between the foam and the top of the container with pieces of lichen held in place with bent medium-gauge stub wires.

1 Use the knife to cut the block of floral foam to fit the container. The foam should sit about 2.5 cm (1 in) below the top of the container.

2 Trim the assegai sticks to 60 cm (24 in).

3 Push about a quarter of the length of the assegai sticks into the centre of the floral foam in the container.

4 Use the secateurs to remove the heads from the bulrushes, leaving about 5 cm (2 in) of stem. Trim eight of the thick-stemmed reeds to 28 cm (11 in), and eight to 25 cm (10 in).

5 Push the bulrush heads into the foam in a circle around the assegai sticks.

harvest moon

As a symbol of the continuity of life, wreaths play a part in many
different cultures. In the autumn, when we are celebrating the
gathering in of the harvest and Thanksgiving, a wreath makes
a particularly appropriate floral decoration, and what better
materials to use than the wheat and grasses of field and meadow?
Mellow orange marigolds and yellow roses give a splash
of colour, while hessian bows suit the rustic theme.

materials & equipment

wire wreath frame, 60 cm (24 in) diameter

8–10 large handfuls of hay

90–100 stems dried wheat

50 dried marigolds

20–30 dried yellow roses

wire cutters • reel wire • secateurs • medium-gauge stub wires • glue
approximately 2.5 m (3 yd) x 2.5 cm (1 in) hessian ribbon • heavy-gauge stub wires

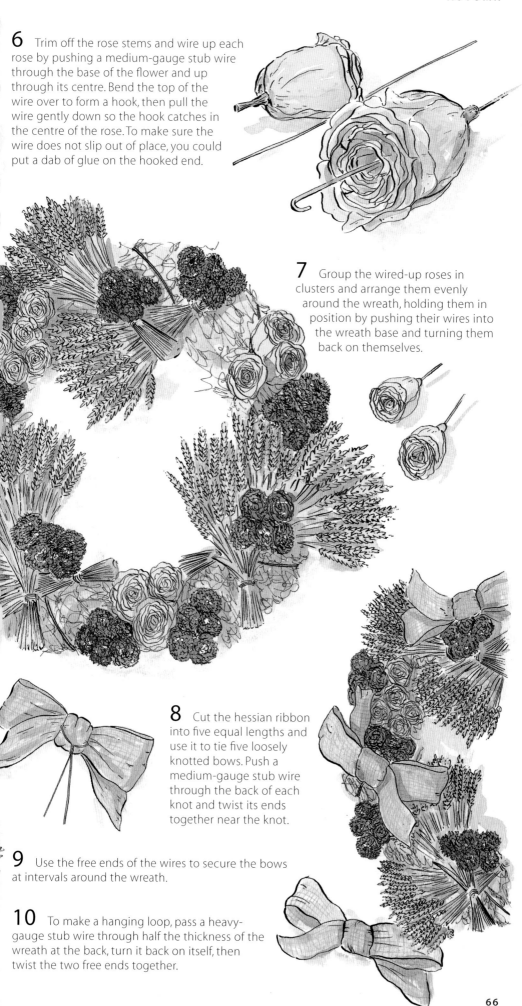

6 Trim off the rose stems and wire up each rose by pushing a medium-gauge stub wire through the base of the flower and up through its centre. Bend the top of the wire over to form a hook, then pull the wire gently down so the hook catches in the centre of the rose. To make sure the wire does not slip out of place, you could put a dab of glue on the hooked end.

7 Group the wired-up roses in clusters and arrange them evenly around the wreath, holding them in position by pushing their wires into the wreath base and turning them back on themselves.

8 Cut the hessian ribbon into five equal lengths and use it to tie five loosely knotted bows. Push a medium-gauge stub wire through the back of each knot and twist its ends together near the knot.

9 Use the free ends of the wires to secure the bows at intervals around the wreath.

10 To make a hanging loop, pass a heavy-gauge stub wire through half the thickness of the wreath at the back, turn it back on itself, then twist the two free ends together.

1 To make a base for the wreath, form the hay into bundles and hold the bundles together by wrapping reel wire around them. Attach the hay to the wire wreath frame at intervals using more pieces of reel wire.

2 Trim the stems of wheat to about 20 cm (8 in) and wrap them in six clusters using medium-gauge stub wires. Twist the wires together to hold the wheat securely, leaving the ends free.

3 Lay the wheat clusters on the wreath base, positioning them at even intervals and arranging them so their heads point alternately inwards and outwards. Push their wires into the base and turn each one back on itself to secure.

4 Use medium-gauge stub wires to wire up ten bunches of five marigolds.

5 Position and secure the bunches of marigolds on the wreath, arranging them between the clusters of wheat.

out of africa

This design makes me think of a piece of sculpted African wood.
To see it at its best, try standing it on a tall plinth where it can
dominate a room. Colour is the keynote. The tiered dark mahogany
raffia fruits and fiery burnt orange proteas pack a punch and
underline the rich warmth of the terracotta container. Stems
of fasciated willow zoom wildly out of the top with
the energy of a rhythmic tribal dance.

materials & equipment

container, 37 x 18 x 18 cm (15 x 7 x 7 in)

1 block dry floral foam, 55 x 32 x 23 cm (22 x 13 x 9 in)

8–10 stems fasciated willow

20–25 dried proteas

15–20 dried raffia fruits

knife • secateurs

4 Insert the proteas in the foam in a circle around the fasciated willow.

5 Trim the raffia fruits to 25 cm (10 in).

6 Insert the raffia fruits around the edge of the container and fill any gaps between the raffia fruits and the proteas with more proteas.

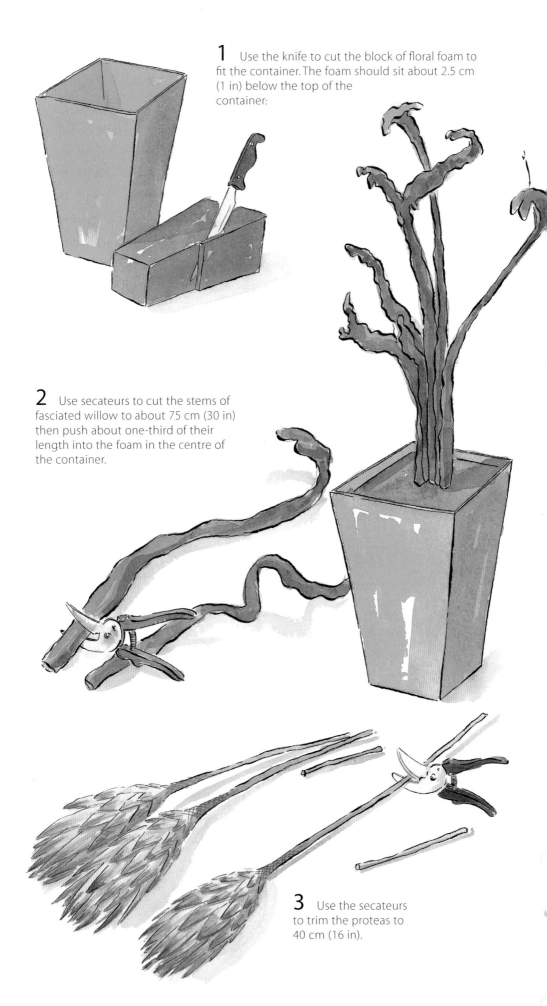

1 Use the knife to cut the block of floral foam to fit the container. The foam should sit about 2.5 cm (1 in) below the top of the container:

2 Use secateurs to cut the stems of fasciated willow to about 75 cm (30 in) then push about one-third of their length into the foam in the centre of the container.

3 Use the secateurs to trim the proteas to 40 cm (16 in).

kitchen-sink drama

Old wooden kitchen utensils add a surprise element to a classical garland and make it perfect for a traditional country-style kitchen. But it would look spectacular in a contemporary kitchen, too. You can also adapt this idea to personalize it for a special friend. Try a collection of indoor gardening tools for a keen horticulturalist, writing implements for a budding author, or artist's materials for that fledgling Jackson Pollock.

materials & equipment

5cm (2 in) chicken wire, 50 cm (20 in) x 105 cm (3 ft 6 in)

dried sphagnum moss, for garland

20-25 preserved ivy leaves

6 assorted wooden kitchen utensils

10–15 dried gourds, 10–12 dried artichokes, 40–45 dried apple slices, 20–25 dried cherry chilli peppers

medium-gauge stub wires • wire cutters • reel wire • knife • heavy-gauge stub wires

7 Make a hole in the base of each gourd with a knife and wire up the gourds using medium-gauge stub wires. Push another stub wire through the lower leaves of each artichoke and twist the ends of the wire together.

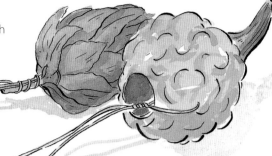

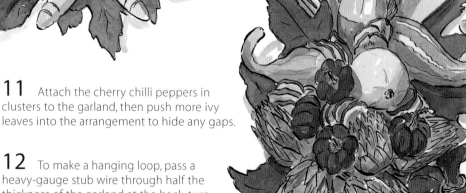

8 Arrange the gourds and artichokes evenly on the moss garland, attaching them in the same way as the utensils.

9 Thread five or six slices of apple together onto a medium-gauge stub wire, twist the ends together and wire them onto the moss garland. Repeat using all the apple slices.

10 Use medium-gauge stub wires to wire up the cherry chilli peppers.

11 Attach the cherry chilli peppers in clusters to the garland, then push more ivy leaves into the arrangement to hide any gaps.

12 To make a hanging loop, pass a heavy-gauge stub wire through half the thickness of the garland at the back, turn it back on itself, then twist the two free ends together.

1 Leaving the edges clear, lay handfuls of moss down the centre of the chicken wire.

2 Fold the edges of the chicken wire over to enclose the moss, forming a moss garland. Flatten the garland by stamping on it.

3 Bend medium-gauge stub wires into hairpin shapes with one end longer than the other, and use to wire up each ivy leaf.

4 Attach the ivy leaves around the edges and down the centre of the moss garland by pushing their wires through the garland and turning them back on themselves to secure.

5 Wire up the wooden kitchen utensils by wrapping reel wire tightly round them, leaving the long ends of wire free.

6 Position the utensils on the moss garland, and attach them using the long ends of wire.

winter

Keep it cool, keep it simple, keep it chic. When the colourful, glitzy excesses of the festive season start to pall, a dash of authentic winter spirit is the antidote you need. Forget all the forced brightness of Christmas. Instead, dig in for a new ice age. Excavate earth-chilled, ice-cracked mineral tones of slate, charcoal, white and silver, then mould and freeze them into frosty, clean-edged designs to strike a chill in your heart.

above left Take two classic glass urns, fill with dried lavender and rich red roses, and you have a Christmas table centre that is distinctively contemporary and extremely stylish. For the evening, surround the vases with glowing red glass nightlights, and dress up each of your guests' napkins with a sprig of dried lavender and a dried red rose.

above right Arctic-cool, pure glacial white flowers are hard to find in nature, but these freeze-dried roses come close. Their tissue-like texture has a fairy-tale magic that is hard to beat, especially set against the shiny smooth chunky creamware pot and the flowing grain of a pale wood table.

left Dried lotus seed heads have such an unusual structure, you could be forgiven for thinking they are some early, primitive life-form. That makes them prime candidates for combining with a wonderful organic pumice-stone pot, as if the two have risen from the depths of a primeval swamp.

above Winter evergreens like this blue-grey preserved juniper are a great treat when there are few fresh flowers to be had. With its complex leaf form and luscious dangling bunches of berries, it needs no embellishment other than to be made up into a simple, welcoming wreath.

left This shimmery, silvery pot looks unique but is unbelievably simple to copy. Just paint a pot silver, then give it a loose wash of white paint over the top. The solidly packed poppy seed heads have been spray-painted silver in sympathy. To double the impact, do as I have, and stand the whole thing in front of a mirror.

cone confection

Whatever the setting, traditional or contemporary, this cone
sculpture will fit the bill. Make the most of the different colours
and forms of the cones by arranging them in bold bands as I have
done. The layers of cones in the urn are magnified by the glass,
giving them an extra dimension that I love. Don't you just feel
like curling up in front of the fire on a winter's evening
with this rustic, nut-brown companion?

materials & equipment

glass urn, 50 cm (20 in) high x 28 cm (11 in) diameter

450–500 assorted pine and fir cones in four different sizes

1 block dry floral foam, 55 x 32 x 23 cm (22 x 13 x 9 in)

1 dry floral foam cone, 60 cm (24 in) high x 21 cm (8½ in) diameter

wooden stick, 60 cm (24 in) long x 2.5 cm (1 in) diameter

knife • ruler • pencil • glue • medium-gauge stub wires

7 Glue a row of medium-sized cones around the top of the band of long, narrow cones, and another row along the upper scored line. Fill between the two rows with more medium-sized cones.

8 Fill to the top of the foam cone with the smallest cones.

9 Wire up the largest cones by weaving a medium-gauge stub wire between their lower scales, then twisting the two ends of the wire together.

10 Finish by pushing the wired-up cones into the bottom of the foam cone, making a loose circle of cones to conceal the top of the glass urn.

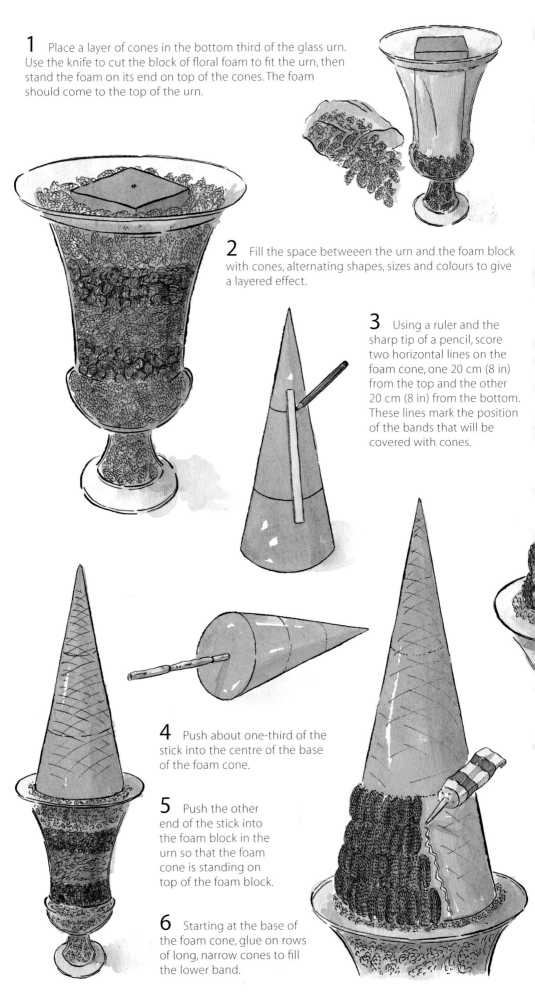

1 Place a layer of cones in the bottom third of the glass urn. Use the knife to cut the block of floral foam to fit the urn, then stand the foam on its end on top of the cones. The foam should come to the top of the urn.

2 Fill the space betweeen the urn and the foam block with cones, alternating shapes, sizes and colours to give a layered effect.

3 Using a ruler and the sharp tip of a pencil, score two horizontal lines on the foam cone, one 20 cm (8 in) from the top and the other 20 cm (8 in) from the bottom. These lines mark the position of the bands that will be covered with cones.

4 Push about one-third of the stick into the centre of the base of the foam cone.

5 Push the other end of the stick into the foam block in the urn so that the foam cone is standing on top of the foam block.

6 Starting at the base of the foam cone, glue on rows of long, narrow cones to fill the lower band.

82

fiery but fun

This has to be my favourite kitchen arrangement. You feel as if you could just pick off a chilli pepper or two to use in your latest Thai recipe. But I don't advise it. The wire urn container is fun, too. It looks very kitcheny, so is ideal for this design. The dyed moss is not only lovely to look at, but helps to hide the foam holding the stem in place. And if you get tired of the chilli pepper tree, you can always fill the wire urn with fresh fruit and vegetables.

materials & equipment

wire urn, 25 cm (10 in) high x 20 cm (8 in) diameter

1 block dry floral foam, 55 x 32 x 23 cm (22 x 13 x 9 in)

dried reindeer moss, dyed rust colour, to fill

wooden stick, 50 cm (20 in) long x 1.5 cm (½ in) diameter

1 ball dry floral foam, 12 cm (5 in) diameter

14–16 stems red dogwood

200–220 dried chilli peppers

knife • glue • medium-gauge stub wires

5 Wire the remaining chilli peppers by pushing a medium-gauge stub wire through the tip of each pepper. Bring the ends of the wire together and twist them around one another.

6 Cover the foam ball with the wired-up chilli peppers, distributing those wired through their tip evenly among the others.

7 Cover the top of the foam in the urn with more clumps of coloured moss, held in place with bent stub wires.

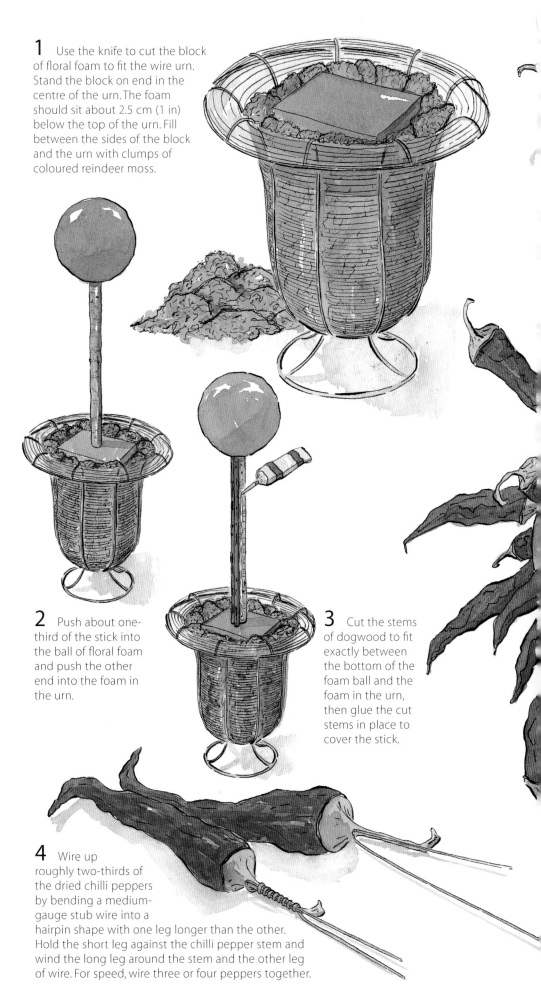

1 Use the knife to cut the block of floral foam to fit the wire urn. Stand the block on end in the centre of the urn. The foam should sit about 2.5 cm (1 in) below the top of the urn. Fill between the sides of the block and the urn with clumps of coloured reindeer moss.

2 Push about one-third of the stick into the ball of floral foam and push the other end into the foam in the urn.

3 Cut the stems of dogwood to fit exactly between the bottom of the foam ball and the foam in the urn, then glue the cut stems in place to cover the stick.

4 Wire up roughly two-thirds of the dried chilli peppers by bending a medium-gauge stub wire into a hairpin shape with one leg longer than the other. Hold the short leg against the chilli pepper stem and wind the long leg around the stem and the other leg of wire. For speed, wire three or four peppers together.

83

glacial ice-cap

Cool and icy, a ball of lichen perched on top of a classic glass urn
filled with reindeer moss looks likes an ice-age fossil preserved in
permafrost. Suiting either the clean lines of a steel and glass
interior or a classic room decked out with marble or limestone,
it cries out to be touched. Underline its tactile quality, exquisite
texture and subtle black and grey shading by standing
it beneath the light of a lamp.

materials & equipment

glass urn, 40 cm (16 in) high x 20 cm (8 in) diameter

dried grey reindeer moss, to fill

1 block dry floral foam, 55 x 32 x 23 cm (22 x 13 x 9 in)

wooden stick, 30 cm (12 in) long x 1.5 cm (½ in) diameter

1 ball dry floral foam, 20 cm (8 in) diameter

dried grey lichen, to cover

knife • glue

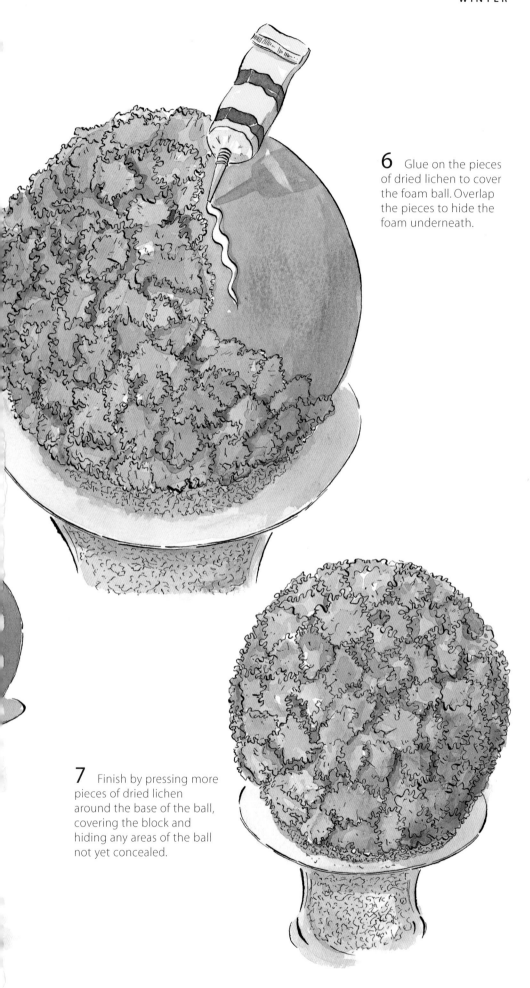

6 Glue on the pieces of dried lichen to cover the foam ball. Overlap the pieces to hide the foam underneath.

7 Finish by pressing more pieces of dried lichen around the base of the ball, covering the block and hiding any areas of the ball not yet concealed.

1 Place a layer of dried reindeer moss in the bottom third of the glass urn and press the moss down firmly.

2 Use the knife to cut the block of floral foam to fit into the vase on top of the moss. Taper the block so that it fits into the body of the vase.

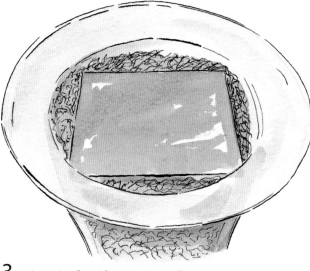

3 Place the floral foam on top of the reindeer moss so that it sits about 2.5 cm (1 in) below the mouth of the urn. Fill the space between the foam and the sides of the urn with more reindeer moss.

4 Push about one-third of the stick into the ball of floral foam.

5 Push the rest of the stick, with the ball attached, into the floral foam so the ball is resting on top of the block.

instructions under flap ➤

the midas touch

You don't have to be a wizard to make a magical display like this one. All it takes is a glass bowl and some imagination. Although the bowl actually holds all the different elements, it is the gold that unites their varied shapes and textures. A quick spray of paint could transform it from gold to silver which would look equally attractive. Don't forget to use a flame-retardant spray before you light the candles!

materials & equipment

glass bowl, 15 cm (6 in) high x 30 cm (12 in) diameter

1 block dry floral foam, 25 x 29 x 12 cm (10 x 11½ x 5 in)

3 candles, 20 cm (8 in) high x 6 cm (2½ in) diameter

5–6 small handfuls of dried grass

8–10 medium handfuls of dried lichen

10–15 stems willow, 60 cm (24 in) long

8–10 seppecioa husks

15 gold-painted cane cones

6–9 stems gold-painted ting-ting reed

10–15 gold panchu-reed balls

knife • 15 heavy-gauge stub wires • pebbles • paper • gold spray-paint
flame-retardant spray • medium-gauge stub wires • cloves • star anise • gold glitter

6   Push the cane cones into the top of the foam in clusters of three, ensuring that when the candles are lit and burn down, the cane cones will not be near the flames.

7   Divide the willow into three clusters and use medium-gauge stub wires to tie them together at each end.

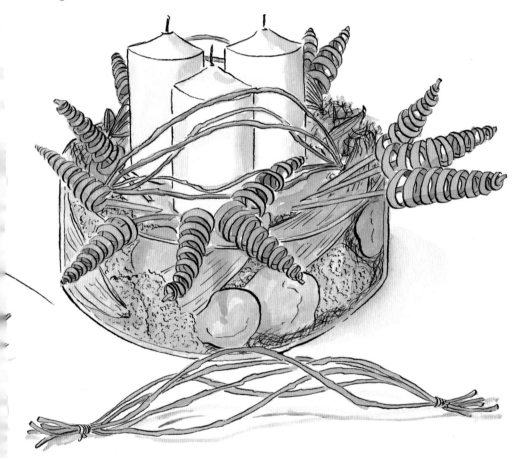

8   Arrange the willow clusters in the foam so they form loose loops. Ensure that the willow does not get in the way of the candle flames.

9   Arrange three clusters of ting-ting reed around the edges of the bowl.

10   Scatter the panchu-reed balls, cloves and star anise over the top of the arrangement, then finish with a sprinkling of gold glitter.

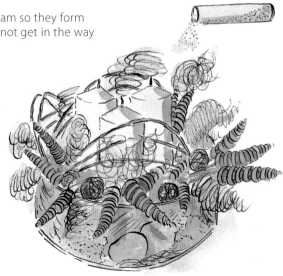

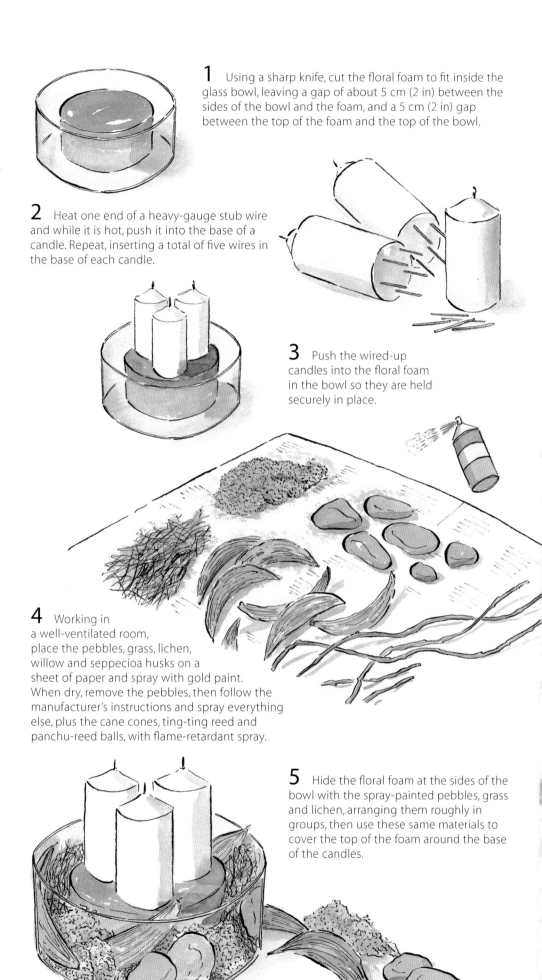

1 Using a sharp knife, cut the floral foam to fit inside the glass bowl, leaving a gap of about 5 cm (2 in) between the sides of the bowl and the foam, and a 5 cm (2 in) gap between the top of the foam and the top of the bowl.

2 Heat one end of a heavy-gauge stub wire and while it is hot, push it into the base of a candle. Repeat, inserting a total of five wires in the base of each candle.

3 Push the wired-up candles into the floral foam in the bowl so they are held securely in place.

4 Working in a well-ventilated room, place the pebbles, grass, lichen, willow and seppecioa husks on a sheet of paper and spray with gold paint. When dry, remove the pebbles, then follow the manufacturer's instructions and spray everything else, plus the cane cones, ting-ting reed and panchu-reed balls, with flame-retardant spray.

5 Hide the floral foam at the sides of the bowl with the spray-painted pebbles, grass and lichen, arranging them roughly in groups, then use these same materials to cover the top of the foam around the base of the candles.

bed of roses

Arrangements in baskets give the impression that someone has simply walked around the garden with the basket over their arm, filling it with flowers as they go. And in the depths of winter, what better way to create a romantic summery feeling than with a mass of dried red roses piled up in a basket? The pine cones and preserved foliage add the wintery touch that makes this a perfect display for the festive season.

materials & equipment

woven basket, 12 cm (5 in) high x 37cm (15 in) diameter

65–75 pine cones

5 blocks dry floral foam, 23 x 11 x 8 cm (9 x 4½ x 3¼ in)

45–55 sprigs preserved juniper

160–170 dried red roses

90–100 stems dried red spray roses

medium-gauge stub wires • knife • floristry scissors

6 Push the juniper sprigs into the floral foam to form a deep band around the top of the pine cones.

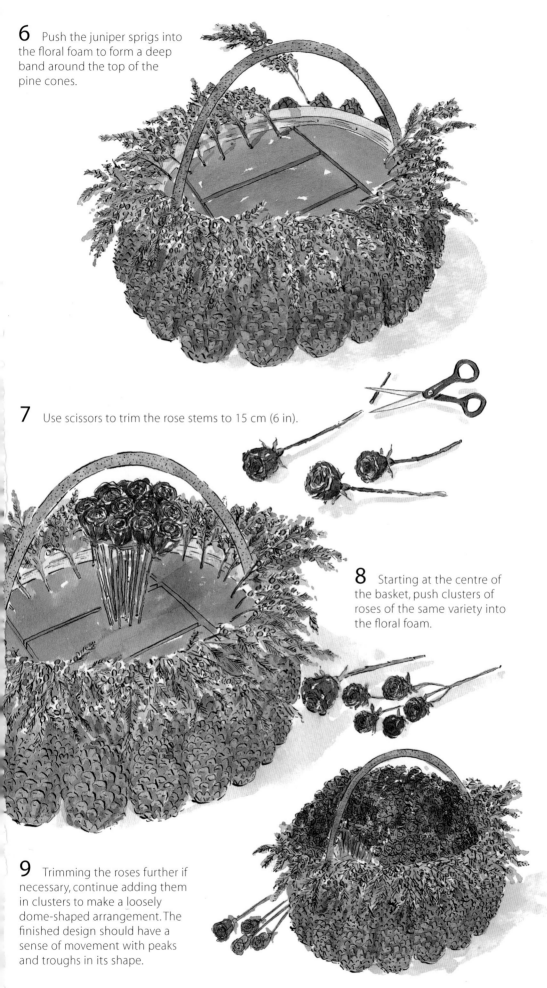

7 Use scissors to trim the rose stems to 15 cm (6 in).

8 Starting at the centre of the basket, push clusters of roses of the same variety into the floral foam.

9 Trimming the roses further if necessary, continue adding them in clusters to make a loosely dome-shaped arrangement. The finished design should have a sense of movement with peaks and troughs in its shape.

1 Wire up the pine cones by weaving a medium-gauge stub wire between the lowest row of scales to form a circle of wire around the bottom of each cone.

2 Wire a circle of cones around the base of the basket, pushing the wires in and out of the weave of the basket and twisting them to hold the pine cones in place.

3 Wire a second row of pine cones above the first.

4 Use the knife to cut the blocks of floral foam to fit inside the basket.

5 Trim the sprigs of preserved juniper to remove any foliage from the lower part of the stems.

traditional containers

Many of the containers I use can be classified as traditional in style. Among my favourites are those made of toleware, a type of enamelled or lacquered metalware popular in the eighteenth century. Without doubt these would look great with a mixed dried arrangement in a traditional room, but they also work well in contemporary mode, filled with a mass of one flower – dried lavender or dried peonies for instance.

Urns are another great classic, either in metal or glass, as here, or in stone or terracotta. Dried mixed flowers in autumnal shades would be suitably traditional in the rusty metal urn, or you can opt for the unexpected by filling the glass urn with dried lichen and placing a lichen ball on top, as I have done on pages 86–88.

People always associate basketware with dried flowers. Baskets can be purchased made from a range of different willows, from light or dark wood, either peeled or left natural, or painted or dyed in different colours. One of my favourite Christmas arrangements is a traditional log basket in a fireplace, filled with silver-birch twigs, pine logs or cones.

In the same vein are containers covered with dried material – twigs such as willow or birch, vines of honeysuckle, or boxwood, eucalyptus or magnolia foliage. These unique containers are fairly easy to make at home and look great filled with dried flowers or foliage. A wooden frame with chicken-wire panels also has a nice country feel, but with a modern edge

to it. If you use one of these, you will have to line it with moss or perhaps with a toning fabric glued in place on the inside of the wooden frame.

I will never tire of using terracotta pots, especially old, weathered ones. You can't beat their warmth and texture and the feeling that they have been lovingly and productively used for many years. The old square French terracotta pot shown here is a variation on the theme. Its top is rimmed with a coloured glaze which gives it a rather modern feel. I like to fill these pots with dried lavender, all trimmed to the same length to give a tabletop effect.

Blue and white china is another classic. It first became popular when examples of plates and vases were shipped to Europe from the Far East, and was then copied endlessly by, among others, the

Dutch, at their factories in Delft. Blue and white china bricks and vases specially designed to hold then-rare specimens of tulip were particularly sought-after. Today, choose blue and white china for traditional arrangements of blue, white and cream dried flowers.

And finally, there are the collectables, like my favourite curvaceous Constance Spry creamware vase, or the chipped old blown-glass vase in its wire frame. It would be foolish to try and fill some of these old vases with water, but with arrangements of dried flowers, you don't need to worry.

modern containers

There has never been a better time for finding stunning modern containers. Used as interior-design accessories in their own right, they come in every imaginable material – glass, terracotta, metal, porcelain, wood, plastic – and every colour of the rainbow. Shops and department stores are full of well-designed, mass-produced examples, while talented artists make collectable one-offs.

Modern containers sit well with my clean, crisp style of dried flower arranging and they suit the dried exotic plant material that is now on the market. My rule is to keep the arrangement simple and let the vase do the talking. Some of the containers pictured here need nothing more than a few stems of silver-grey furry pussy willow, or some funky-looking dried papyrus grass to turn them into a satisfying display.

Plain glass vases are a challenge since the contents of the body of the vase are on show as much as what is in the top. This is where dried fillers can come in useful – for instance, pot-pourri, lavender, preserved fruits, or mosses. According to your taste, choose a contrasting or toning filler.

I love using modern brightly coloured opaque glass vases. They come in all shapes and sizes and have very strong personalities, so it's best to work with them, not against them. Try green thistles and dyed green lichen in a green vase, or blue-grey eucalyptus or blue-tinged hydrangeas in a blue one.

Although people usually associate terracotta with old, rose-covered country cottages, it also comes in new designs with modern proportions. And it is a

particularly good material to use in a contemporary setting where organic materials set the tone.

Metal containers are very much in keeping with today's interiors. I love them in nickel, chrome or fashionably galvanized, and those with textured finishes are even more appealing. Try filling them with a mass of freeze-dried roses. I think the juxtaposition of the modern and the traditional is really exciting.

Today's porcelain comes in some lovely shapes and colours, though, personally, I prefer using white. My favourites are sexily curved. I think they look great with blowsy dried peonies or with clusters of roses.

Well-finished wooden containers make unusual additions to contemporary rooms. I especially like using dark wood. It looks amazing with dried snakegrass or papyrus and would definitely suit an east-meets-west-type of interior.

Plastics are, of course, the great discovery of the modern era. I think today's most interesting plastic containers are the square or rectangular ones made from clear or frosted perspex. Available in different sizes, they are so designworthy that you don't need to be especially talented to make a beautiful arrangement in them. Simply fill with matching dried flower or seed heads, and let Nature do the rest.

left Artichokes are one of the most sculptural dried plants I use but because they are so dominant, they often look best on their own: in a mixed arrangement they can be overpowering. I love their spiky purple tops and maroon petals. They look great simply *en masse* in a tall vase, or I like making them up into wreaths – just the lovely fat heads tightly packed next to one another, nothing more.

below Sweetcorn is the epitome of harvest-time, so I prefer to use it at that season. You can make it into attractive wreaths or you could just tie several stems together with raffia and use them as a wall decoration in the kitchen. For an autumn dinner-party, use a small sweetcorn tied to a napkin for each of your guests. They look delightful and are sure to please.

right, clockwise Papyrus grass dries to a soft, sage-green, sinuous paintbrush shape. Larkspur comes in shades of pink and mauve. Normally thought of as a softly romantic summer-garden flower, once dried, it looks quite formal and structured. Use it to make geometric, tiered arrangements. This dried papyrus still retains its leaf-like bracts, which give it a wild, rather untamed look. White spray-painted ears of wheat with a hint of gold glitter add a touch of ghostly elegance to a design. Silver glitter looks ethereal, too.

extending the range

Modern methods of drying and preserving plant material are constantly pushing back the boundaries of what can be used. That is great news since it means that there is always some foliage or flower to catch the mood of contemporary interiors. Try some of these old and new favourites for yourself.

top left Tall larkspur makes a good base for a big arrangement. This pink variety looks romantic combined with peonies.

top right Celosia comes in pink through to burgundy. Its dramatic sinuous flowers are effective massed in a terracotta pot.

above Eucalyptus is silver-grey but can be dyed, as here. I like it on its own in a modern container, or wired into a topiary tree.

right Although much used, cream to red-brown helichrysum is still extremely beautiful.

right Dried linseed is a very delicate-looking creature that is pretty on its own or as an edging around a pot. You can also try spraying it gold or silver to add sparkle to an arrangement.

far right Chinese lanterns remind me of my mother who always used them in her mixed dried arrangements. But they have contemporary appeal, too. Thirty or forty stems in a tall wooden vase will look like a piece of modern sculpture. And if the bright colour does not attract you, they can be obtained in a lovely soft green – as they are before the pods turn red.

above Love-in-a-mist is a favourite English country classic of mine. The puffy, light-as-air seed heads dry well and have attractive deep purple markings. They are a great filler for mixed arrangements and tone well with nearly all dried flowers.

above right The seed pods of honesty are better known in their silver form, which is the result of removing their outer beige covering. But these look more modern: they have been dried while still mauve-green.

right I usually think of freeze-dried apple slices as an ingredient for pot-pourri, but they also look pretty piled up on a wooden tray.

right Cedar cones have a beautiful layered appearance and give off a wonderful pine-like fragrance. When dried, they nearly always have a sticky residue on the outside which I think makes them even more attractive. They sometimes shatter into layers. When this happens, I like piling the pieces into a wooden or glass bowl. Simple, but effective.

below These dried cherries simply ooze sweetness. Surprisingly, even after drying, they retain a lot of their colour and shine. Use them to provide a touch of the unexpected in an arrangement.

below Dried fungus looks rather futuristic. It is actually a parasite that grows on trees and branches. I sometimes wire it up into a topiary tree, or spray it gold or silver to use in Christmas arrangements.

below left Dried kumquats look good just on their own, or as an edging to an arrangement. They are expensive, but you only need a few for impact.

below right Lichen can be dyed to almost any colour. Use it to conceal the mechanics of an arrangement, to top off a cement-filled pot, or to fill the body of a glass vase.

a few essentials

Making beautiful arrangements of dried flowers isn't difficult and you don't need an enormous financial outlay to get started, but there are one or two essential tools and materials that it's worth investing in to make life easier. Once you start dried flower arranging, I'm sure that, like me, you'll find it addictive and will want to use everything in sight. You'll be surprised to know that there's a lot of plant material you can dry yourself: I give some advice on how to go about it. And finally, having spent so much time making your arrangements, you'll want to know how to keep them looking good. Follow my tips to see how that can be achieved.

essential tools and equipment

There is a wide range of tools and equipment available for making dried flower arrangements, but those you will find most useful are a pair of high-quality floristry scissors, secateurs and a sharp knife. Use the scissors or secateurs for cutting plant material (secateurs make easier work of cutting heavy stems) and the knife for cutting floral foam to size and shape and for trimming twigs and branches.

The basis for many arrangements of dried flowers is dry floral foam. Floral foam was invented in 1954 but did not become widely available or affordable until the 1970s. It comes in two forms – green for fresh flowers (which must be soaked before use) and grey-brown (so-called 'dry floral foam') for dried. The dry floral foam came on the market in the 1960s. This type of foam must not be soaked. The two are not interchangeable, although they do share some characteristics. For example, both can be cut to shape and size with a sharp knife, and both are sold in a variety of ready-made shapes. The most common shapes are blocks and balls, which come in several different sizes. Dry floral foam is also available in rings, cones and cylinders.

Some arrangements of dried flowers use a combination of chicken wire and dried moss as their foundation. The moss is wrapped up in the chicken wire to make what I call a 'moss garland'. This can be used on its own, for instance to make a hanging garland (see pages 38–40 and 72–74), or it can provide support for flowers or other material around the edge of a basket (see page 35). A moss garland can also be bent into shape for special effect (see pages 50–52).

Chicken wire is also used to reinforce floral foam in topiary work where the foam is not supported by a container. The chicken wire is available in different gauges, but I find that fine-gauge wire provides the best support for massed flowers. You can also use chicken wire simply crumpled into a container to support flowers and foliage.

Some stiffer plant stems can be placed directly in dry floral foam, but finer stems often need to be wired, as do single leaves, clusters of flowers or foliage, fruits, vegetables and cones, and extras such as shells (see page 35) or wooden accessories (see page 73). Wiring is also useful when finishing off a very densely packed arrangement: it is often easier to slip a few wired-up stems into a tiny space than to try and force in a stem which may snap in the process (see page 26). And wiring is a must for attaching material to a wire-covered moss garland.

The choice of wire is bewildering, but the basic types are stub wires and reel wire. Stub wires come in different lengths and thicknesses ranging from fine to heavy gauge. Use fine wire for delicate flowers and foliage and thicker wire for woody stems, fruits, vegetables and accessories, as well as for making hanging loops at the back of wreaths and garlands. You will need reel wire for binding work in wreaths and garlands.

Floristry scissors will cut through many dried materials, but for twigs or stems, like this contorted willow, you will need secateurs.

Medium-gauge stub wires can be used to wire up fruits and pine cones.

When wiring a shell to make an 'anchor' for other shells in the arrangement, use a combination of wire and glue for greater stability.

In arrangements where the floral foam is not in a container, it will need some reinforcement. Use chicken wire wrapped around the floral foam, cutting into the chicken wire if necessary with wire cutters to ensure a good fit. For extra strength, use more wire to bind the chicken wire to the supporting twigs or pole.

You may be able to cut the finer wire with floristry scissors. Otherwise wire cutters are essential. You may also find pliers useful when it comes to bending thick wires or chicken wire into shape.

Dried flowers are often made into wreaths, and for these you can either make your own wreath frame or buy one ready-made. Home-made frames can be constructed by bending flexible stems such as willow, dogwood or vine, and binding them at intervals with reel wire. Frames made of natural materials can be purchased ready-made, but bought frames are more commonly made of wire to which you bind your own moss, hay or straw, using reel wire.

Glue is another essential for arrangements of dried flowers. You will need it to attach flower heads or moss to foam, to fix decorative twigs to wooden sticks to make topiary tree stems, to cover small areas of the 'mechanics' of an arrangement with moss or other material, and to fix shells (see page 35), rope (see page 43) or other accessories. It is also sometimes useful to add a dab of glue to give extra support to a wired-up flower head, especially if the flower has been wired by pushing a single wire through the head and bending it over at the top (see page 66). Use fast-drying, clear glue. If you prefer, you can use a glue-gun, which is very quick and effective. But take care as the liquid glue is hot.

Quick-drying cement is used to support the stems of topiary trees. Place the cement in an inner container and then put this in an outer, display pot. This is a precautionary measure: as the cement dries, it can sometimes crack the pot.

Spray paint is useful, too, either to add some gold or silver festive glamour to an arrangement or, in green, to colour boxwood foliage. Without a spray of green, boxwood dries out rather quickly to an unappealing dull grey-green colour.

other decorative materials

Among the most common additional decorative materials for dried flower arrangements are moss and lichen. In addition to using these for moss garland

bases (see above), they are invaluable for hiding the mechanics of an arrangement, whether that be the floral foam, chicken wire or cement. There are several different types of moss – bun moss, which grows in small mounds, Spanish moss, with long grey-green strands, grass-like sphagnum moss, the most common type of moss, reindeer moss, which comes in cotton-wool-like clumps, and lichen with its unusual silver-grey wiry clusters. These are just a few of the possibilities. Many of these different mosses can also be purchased dyed to different colours, so you can choose moss to harmonize or contrast with your arrangement.

I also sometimes like to use decorative bows and ties to finish an arrangement or to wrap around bundles of material such as twigs or cinnamon sticks. For preference I would use natural raffia, coarse string or hessian ribbon: their texture and colour make the perfect complement to the dried flowers.

If you are using a glass or perspex vase to hold your dried flower arrangement, you will need to hide the mechanics that hold the display in place. There are many attractive possibilities – dried moss of different types, colours and textures (see above), dried leaves, dried lichen, pebbles or gravel, pot-pourri, cones of various types, small shells, dried fruit slices, even coffee beans or red kidney beans.

drying your own materials

Although there is now an increasingly wide choice of shop-bought dried flowers and foliage available, it can be fun and very rewarding to dry your own. The flowers, leaves and seed heads of nearly every plant can be dried and preserved.

Air-drying is the simplest and most commonly used method of drying at home. Simply hang fresh plant materials upside-down in bunches and store them in a dry, cool (no less than 10°C, 50°F) room with freely circulating air. Make sure flower heads and foliage are not too close together or the air will not be able to circulate freely and this will cause the petals and leaves to rot. The conditions in an airing cupboard, spare room, attic or loft, garage or shed may be perfect. The results are usually good, with only a small degree of colour fading.

Slices of apple or orange can easily be dried at home in the oven on a low setting. Then they are ready to be threaded on a stub wire and used in an arrangement.

Plant material with large, heavy heads, such as artichokes or sweetcorn, should be supported individually on wire racks. Attach a piece of chicken wire horizontally between a pair of wooden battens and slot each stem through the mesh.

When the materials are thoroughly dry, store them in large cardboard boxes or bags until they are ready to use. Delicate flowers such as roses should be carefully wrapped in newspaper or tissue paper before being stored in a box. Avoid using plastic bags to store any dried plant material as it may become moist and the dried flowers and leaves will rot.

You can also dry some material by simply standing it upright in a vase. This is another variation on air-drying. Tall grasses dry well using this method. Some flowers – among them baby's breath, hydrangeas and delphiniums – do best if you stand them in about 5 cm (2 in) of water. The stems will absorb some water first then, as the water evaporates from the vase, they will slowly dry out.

I love using pine, spruce and fir cones in my dried flower arrangements. These start to dry out while they are still on the tree, but if you collect fallen cones from the ground, all you have to do to complete the drying process is spread them out at room temperature in a single layer on a plate or piece of newspaper for a few days.

Another drying method is to preserve plant material using glycerine. This works best with individual leaves. Its advantage is that the leaves remain supple, but the disadvantage is that there is significant colour loss. Make a solution of half glycerine and half water and immerse the leaves in it for several days, after which they will have changed colour. Remove them from the solution, rinse in a mild solution of detergent, and leave to dry flat on a piece of paper.

Plant material can also be dried using a dessicant which draws out the moisture. Choose from silica gel crystals or borax or alum mixed with fine, dry silver sand. Silica gel crystals can be used repeatedly. Place a 1.5 cm (½ in) layer in the bottom of a wide jar or biscuit tin and place the flower heads on top. Gently brush the crystals between the petals and then over them so the flowers are held in their natural shape. When the flowers are covered, seal the jar or tin and set it aside. After a couple of days, check if the flowers are dry and if they are, remove immediately or they will become brittle. Follow the same procedure for

drying with borax or alum mixed with silver sand (three parts borax or alum to two parts sand). This procedure will take at least ten days.

Finally, you may like to try drying plant material in your oven. Apple, orange, grapefruit, lemon and lime slices respond especially well to this. Cut them into 5 mm (¼ in) slices and spread them out in a single layer on a baking sheet. Dry them in a cool oven at 110°C (225° F) Gas Mark ¼ for about 2–2½ hours, turning them over half-way through the process.

anchoring candles
There are several different methods of anchoring candles in floral foam. The simplest is to heat several stub wires over a flame and, while they are still hot, insert them in the base of the candle so their ends protrude. Ensure that you hold the wire in gloved fingers or in a pair of pliers to prevent getting burned as the wire heats up.

Other methods of anchoring candles involve using florist's tape to attach bent stub wires, matchsticks or lengths of wooden skewer around the base of the candle, leaving the ends protruding.

maintaining dried flower arrangements
Dried flowers are easily spoiled by adverse environmental conditions, but they can last for months, and sometimes even for years. Some will last longer than others, some colours will take on an antiqued look, while others will never change. The general rule is to keep them out of the kitchen and bathroom where the naturally moist environment can cause the plant materials to deteriorate. Only dark-coloured freeze-dried roses appear to benefit from humid conditions. Try also to keep the arrangements away from direct heat or sunlight, which cause the colour of the flowers and foliage to fade.

Most importantly, never put dried flowers near an open fire and if the arrangement includes candles, you must protect it with a fire-retardant spray (see page 91 and Suppliers, pages 110-111).

Finally, you can waft a hairdryer over dried flower arrangements at regular intervals to prevent household dust from gathering on leaves and petals.

suppliers

Dried flowers and foliage, and dried arrangements

Large department stores often stock a good selection of dried flowers and seed heads.

A & F Bacon Ltd.
253/254 Flower Market
New Covent Garden Market
Nine Elms
London SW8 5NA
Tel: 0171 720 1843
Suppliers of pine cones

C. Best
Unit P50-55 Flower Market
New Covent Garden Market
Nine Elms
London SW8
Tel: 0171 720 2306
Fresh flowers as well as dried roses and dried wheat and grasses.

Cameron-Shaw
279 New Kings Road
London SW6 4RD
Tel: 0171 371 8175
Retailers of preserved and dried flowers, and dried flower arrangements made to order.

The Conservatory Flower Shop
13 Brewer's Lane
Richmond
Surrey
TW9 1HH
Tel: 0181 940 2265
A comprehensive range of dried flowers.

Elmtree Dried Flowers
Elmtree Farm
Frocester Stonehouse
Gloucester
GL10 3TG
Tel: 01453 823274
Stocks a wide range of dried

flowers and floristry equipment and tools. Mail order available. Holds one-day courses and evening classes in dried flower arranging. Phone for details and brochure.

Lesley Hart Dried Flowers
37 Smith Street
Warwick
CV34 4JA
Tel: 01926 490 356
Retailers of a wide selection of dried flowers and foliage.

Pulbrook and Gould
Liscartan House
127 Sloane Street
London SW1X 9AS
Tel: 0171 730 0030
Dried flower arrangements made to order.

Something Special
Stand A1 Flower Market
New Covent Garden Market
Nine Elms
London SW8 5NA
Tel: 0171 720 3466
A wide range of dried flowers and florist's sundries.

Moyses Stevens Ltd.
157 Sloane Street
London SW1X 9BT
Tel: 0171 259 9303
Dried flower arrangements made to order.

Kenneth Turner
125 Mount Street
London W1 Y5HA
Tel: 0171 355 3880
Dried flower arrangements made to order.

Woodhams Ltd
One Aldwych
London WC2 4BZ
Tel: 0171 300 0777
Dried flower arrangements made to order.

Florist's equipment and sundries

Local garden centres are a wonderful source for most florist's equipment, including floral foam, containers, baskets, troughs, wires, ribbons and string.

B & Q
Branches nationwide; for nearest branch, phone 0181 466 4166
Stocks a good selection of tools and florist's sundries, such as secateurs.

Diddybox
132-134 Belmont Road
Astley Bridge
Bolton
BL1 7AN
Tel: 01204 595610
Flower arranger's sundries.

Donovan Brothers
165 Childers Street
Deptford
London SE8 5JU
Tel: 0171 720 5417
Suppliers of florist's sundries including dry floral foam, wires, etc.

Vince Durrant
W. Hogewoning BV
P.O. Box 600
Allington
Maidston
Kent
ME16 0GZ
Tel: 01622 664 881
Trendsetters in floral decorations.

The Flower Arrangers' Show Shop
P.O. Box 38
Stratford-upon-Avon
Warwicks.
CV37 6WJ
Florist's sundries. Mail order.

Homebase
Branches nationwide; for nearest
branch, phone 0645 801 800
Some dried flowers; gardening
tools and bamboo canes; florist's
sundries including dry floral foam,
tape and wires.

Smithers-Oasis UK Ltd.
Crowther Road
Crowther Industrial Estate
Washington
Tyne & Wear
NE38 0AQ
Tel: 0191 417 5595
Manufacturers of accessories for
fresh flower and dried flower
arranging and a range of floral
foam products, including bricks
and wreath frames, in a vast range
of sizes and shapes. Phone for your
local stockist.

Joanna Wood
48a Pimlico Road
London SW1W 8LP
Tel: 0171 730 5064
Decorative accessories, including
pine cones.

Ribbons and trimmings
Local department stores or
haberdasheries usually stock a
good selection of ribbons, string
and decorative ties and trims.

John Lewis Partnership
278-306 Oxford Street
London W1A 1EX
Tel: 0171 629 7711
Suppliers of haberdashery, ribbons,
trimmings and sundries.

J. T Morgan
28 Chepstow Corner
Chepstow Place
London W2 4XA
Tel: 0171 229 1011

V. V. Rouleaux
54 Sloane Square
Cliveden Place
London SW1W 8AX
Tel: 0171 730 3125
Impressive selection of ribbons in
all widths and textures, including
wire-edged ribbon and trimmings.

Shells and stones

Civil Engineering Developments
728 London Road
West Thurrock
Grays
Essex
RM20 3LU
Tel: 01708 867237
Unusual stones and pebbles.

Heiploeg & Lynn Shrimpers
Alexandra Dock
Kings Lynn
Norfolk
PE30 2ET
Tel: 01553 772520
A wide selection of shells.

Candles

The Candle Shop
30 The Market
Covent Garden
London WC2E 8RE
Tel: 0171 836 9815

Carden Cunietti
83 Westbourne Park Road
London W2 5QH
Tel: 0171 229 8559

Price's Patent Candle Co. Ltd.
110 York Road
Battersea
London SW11 3RU
Tel: 0171 228 3345
A grand selection of candles,
including traditional church
candles

Paints
The following shops sell gold
spray paint and other artist's
materials you may find useful.

Fred Aldous
P.O. Box 135
37 Lever Street
Manchester 1
M60 1UX
Tel: 0161 236 2477
Craft materials by mail order.

Specialists Crafts
P.O. Box 247
Leicester
LE1 9AF
Tel: 0116 251 0405
Craft supplies of all types. Mail
order.

Fire-retardant spray

Flamebar Flame Retardants
Flamebar Ltd.
Chestnut Estate
Bassingham
Lincoln
LN5 9LL
Tel: 01522 788818
Highly effective range of water-
based flame retardant sprays to
protect dried natural flowers and
grasses.

Baskets, vases and containers

Woodhams Ltd
One Aldwych
London WC2 4BZ
Tel: 0171 300 0777
Suppliers of creamware, vases, pots
and containers

Accessories
Visit the following stores for stylish
accessories, including china, metal
and glass dishes and vases and
containers, as well as candles.

The Conran Shop
Michelin House
81 Fulham Road
London SW3 6RD
Tel: 0171 589 7401

Habitat
196 Tottenham Court Road
London
W1P 9LD
Tel: 0171 631 3880

Heal's
196 Tottenham Court Road
London W1P 9LD
Tel: 0171 636 1666

IKEA
2 Drury Way
North Circular Road
London NW10 OTH
Tel: 0181 208 5600

The Pier
200 Tottenham Court Road
London W1P 9LA
Tel: 0171 637 7001

The Source
26-40 Kensington High Street
London W8 4PF
Tel: 0171 937 2626

acknowledgements

Firstly, I would like to thank my team at Woodhams Ltd, for their help and support over the past days, weeks, months and years. Without them, nothing would be possible and Woodhams Ltd would not be the successful company it is, nor would it be so enjoyable to work there. In particular, I would like to thank Mark Siredzuk for all he has done to produce the dried flower arrangements in this book, Heather Alexander and Emma Townsend for their continued help with the floral department, and Robin Mellon, my P.A., for his constant assistance in keeping my life running smoothly.

This is also a good opportunity for me to mention Hilary Mandleberg at Ryland, Peters & Small, and to thank her for her dedicated and often time-consuming work and encouragement. I also want to thank Sally Powell, the designer of this book, and Anne Ryland, for all the help they have given me.

I would also like to thank several of our suppliers – Something Special, Tudor Rose and C. Best at New Covent Garden Flower Market, and Peter Harvey in High Wycombe – for constantly providing us with fabulous materials.